DECEIVED

How Christian Arabs Made Islamic Conquests Possible

MOURAD AKESBI

CONTENTS

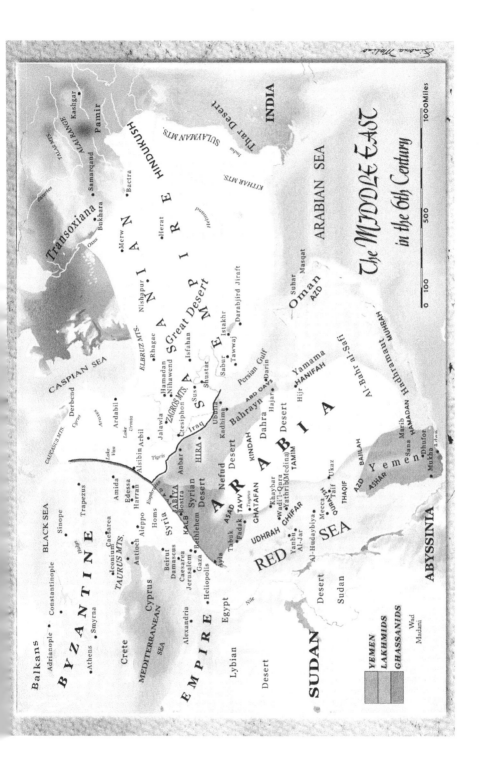

The MIDDLE EAST in the 6th Century

Emma Melia

PROLOGUE

I was born in Morocco in 1960, four years after independence from France. I grew up in a fervent nationalistic environment with calls for annexation of remaining colonized areas, such as Western Sahara and Spanish enclaves of Ceuta and Melilla; self-reliance; and nationalization of large sectors of the economy still controlled by French corporations. This nationalism expressed itself in many ways. In the case of education, it resulted in the publication of textbooks with a nationalistic bent. History textbooks extolled the extraordinary military and cultural achievements of Arabs and described their decline as a direct consequence of the crusades and colonization of the Arab world. I was taught that original Arab strength derived from faith and unity and that to regain it, all we needed was to reclaim those indispensable ingredients.

Nothing came out of unity as each Arab country was fighting another over artificial borders traced by European powers, or some other issue. Arabs were left with the other ingredient, faith. By the eighties, a large section of Arab societies embraced a Salafist brand of Islam in the hope that a faith that appeared to have a golden age about 1,400 years ago might create the same feat again. Some Arabs also accepted violence or jihad as a legitimate means to push back against perceived domination by imperialist neo-colonial powers and their local cronies, whether in Afghanistan, Algeria, or East Africa. Iranians were not immune to this phenomenon as the Islamic Revolution of 1979 made amply clear.

The educational brainwashing that occurred after independence played a significant role in creating the Arab and Muslim malaise we live in today, as several generations of Arabs and Muslims, starting with mine, experienced a frustrating discrepancy between an actual sense of victimhood and inferiority toward the West, and a perceived sense of religious and civilizational superiority as told by the textbooks, the media, and political and religious leaders.

The Arab world, therefore, believed simultaneously in a cult of the hero, built upon a mythologized golden age when Arabs ruled supreme, and a cult of the victim whereupon they believed that most of their current ills derived from Western oppression and imperialism.

Independence achieved mostly after World War II, for a short period of time, suppressed the cult of the victim and emphasized the cult of the hero. In addition to the normal fervor created by the achievement of political independence, this misplaced sense of superiority was fed by the writings of several well-meaning European orientalists of the nineteenth century and their twentieth-century Arab followers who romanticized and aggrandized Arab power and contributions to the sciences and humanities. These orientalists, using mostly Abbasid and later sources, also depicted Arabs as an invincible and unstoppable force during the early years of Islam. It is somewhat natural for Arabs to fall prey to this mythical grandeur and try to recapture it through renewed faith and jihad just like their ancestors supposedly did.

I personally experienced several instances of this false aggrandizement of Arab achievements. One of them occurred in middle school in 1974: our French math teacher got frustrated one day because most of the class could not understand his poor explanation of logarithms. He suddenly exclaimed: "I cannot believe that you Arabs cannot understand a mathematical concept invented by one of your ancestors!" He was, of course, referring to Khwārizmī. The problem is that Khwārizmī was a Persian, born in Khwarazm, in western Central Asia. But he did not know that and neither did we.

There is also a sense among Arabs that God elected them as his chosen people to reveal his final and most perfect message to the world in Arabic. These continuous harangues of past grandeur created generations of Arabs with an exaggerated sense of superiority and "manifest destiny," helping to propel missions of nationalists starting in the '30s and of religious extremists starting in the '80s.

The Arab defeats of 1948 and 1967 at the hands of the original and since rejected chosen people, re-emphasized the cult of the victim which could not be reconciled with the cult of the hero, which is based on the belief of the invincibility of Arabs during Muslim conquests. The only possible answer to this conundrum is that to regain their perceived past invincibility, Arabs needed to recapture the old ways of early Islam which appear to have granted such invincibility. Hence, the further rise and fossilization of Islamism, the form of Islam believed to have been practiced by the Prophet Muhammad and the Rashidun Caliphs.

Having deluded themselves into believing in their religious supremacy, and resulting past cultural and military supremacy, Arabs rejected "alien" Western achievements and therefore missed at least a century of transformational developments which include scientific and technological advancement and the evolution of democratic institutions which made it possible for the individual to think analytically, explore, and invent freely.

The purpose of this book is to focus on the past military supremacy component of the delusion and highlight that peninsular Arabs were not warlike and lacked military skills and numbers, and that the "Prophet's armies" surging out of Arabia were a myth.

Peninsular Arabia's demographics in the early seventh century, absence of national or even tribal political cohesion, disastrous economy and finances, and utter lack of military readiness and culture could not have supported the blitzkrieg that overran the Byzantine and Sasanian Empires, notwithstanding their alleged weaknesses.

This book will also show that the so-called Arab conquest was initiated and made possible not by the fervor of a new faith but rather by the insurrection of Christian Arabs against both the Byzantine and Sasanian Empires following the end of the Byzantine-Sasanian War in 628. I will first analyze a dichotomy between the more numerous and more advanced Fertile Crescent Christian Arabs and their peninsular pagan brethren who were far less numerous and advanced on the eve of the final Byzantine-Sasanian War in 602.

I will then focus on the fact that what was described as Muslim conquest by ninth-century Muslim chroniclers was, in all probability, a massive insurrection of both settled and nomadic Christian Arabs starting in 628 in both Iraq and Syria which triggered, in turn, the wholesale defections of Byzantine and Sasanian military units and the rise of notables and local nobility against their central governments. This was the result of the Sasanian occupation of Syria in the 620s and subsequent wars which resulted in pauperization of both Persian and Byzantine populations as well as a nascent Arab nationalism driven initially by Christian Arabs, the Ghassanids in the Levant and Northwestern Arabia and the Lakhmids in Lower Mesopotamia and Eastern Arabia. The ground was therefore rife for a disruptor, in this case the peninsular Arabs, to take advantage of a historical turn of events.

In establishing that the so-called Muslim conquests were primarily the result of a Christian Arab insurrection, which was morphed by the peninsular Arabs into an occupation of both Iraq and Syria, I hope to provide realistic historical insights that may counterbalance the current Arab cult of the hero, a mental and behavioral disease emphasizing old dogma and violence, which only leads to failure and despair. A realistic and honest reassessment of early Arab history may help under-emphasize a mythologized golden past and focus more on inclusion, acceptance of others, progress, modernity, and innovation. Only then may we be able to shake the shackles that hold us back and aspire to a better future.

HISTORIOGRAPHY AND METHODOLOGY

<hr/>

I will first briefly recap the historiography of early Islam, in general, and the Arab conquests, in particular, before describing my proposed methodology.

Historiography

The first serious attempt undertaken to document the conquests occurred during the Abbasid period, over two centuries after the fact. The Muslim ninth-century chroniclers, who were mostly of Persian origin, such as Ibn Hisham, Tabari (history), and al-Isfahani (Kitab al Aghani), understandably sought to understate the accomplishments of the Syrian Christians and their overlords, the Umayyads. Their stories are full of glorious victories emphasizing the power of well-equipped and well-led huge Arab armies suddenly surging out of the sands of Arabia.

According to them, Islam was carried at breakneck speed from Mecca across the whole Middle East by peninsular Arabs, who then established unified rule over all the lands of the former Persian Empire and in all the southern and eastern provinces of the Byzantine Empire in only a few short years. Peninsular Arabs were victorious everywhere; Khālid ibn al-Walīd was a general who, without any prior experience or knowledge, outfoxed experienced Sasanian and Byzantine generals. Non-Arabs everywhere submitted, converted, or were killed; and Islamic government was imposed everywhere. Christian Arabs are rarely mentioned, and when they are, they are put in the role of impotent supporters of their overlords, the Byzantine and Sasanian Empires, and were crushed with them.

Muslim medieval histories are filled with exaggerations and inaccuracies. Tabari, in the preface to his history, honestly stated that he made no attempt to verify the accounts he relied on and that he was presenting them as is. He concluded by saying that only God knows the truth. All other medieval historians followed the same flawed process, as it was the standard practice. To make things worse, the great majority of these historians worked for the Abbasid state, and therefore their histories were written to the taste of their sponsors.

The second serious attempt was made by European orientalists in the nineteenth century. These historians were under the spell of the Romantic movement, which impacted the way Europeans perceived their own history as well that of others. Past events were rewritten to increase nationalist pride: Chateaubriand, the French writer and historian who founded Romanticism (1768-1848), made medieval Christianity cool again. Orleans Bishop Dupanloup pronounced a fervid panegyric on Joan of Arc in 1849, which culminated in her beatification in 1909, notwithstanding the Entente Cordiale with Britain. Eugène Viollet-le-Duc restored many medieval landmarks, including those which had been damaged or abandoned during the French Revolution, such as Notre Dame Cathedral, the Basilica of Saint Denis, and the medieval city of Carcassonne. Sir Walter Scott in Britain sung the feats of Ivanhoe and Robin Hood, Anglo-Saxon heroes defying Norman oppression.

The combined influence of orientalism and Romanticism created a whole class of painters depicting harems with oversexed languorous Arab females and corresponding powerful virile males. Orientalists such as Gustave Le Bon (1841–1931), whose *La Civilisation des Arabes* of 1884 was translated and extensively read in the Arab world starting in the early twentieth century, described Arabs under such positive light that one unfamiliar with Arabs' plight would have thought they were the world's superpower.

This orientalist romanticism was exacerbated by the colonial competition between France and Britain to carve out the remnants of the Ottoman Empire between them. Hence there was a strong display of Anti-Turk propaganda and lionization of the occupied Arabs, hoping to get in the Arabs' good graces.

France, occupying Algeria in 1830 and Tunisia in 1881, and Britain, occupying Egypt in 1882, claimed to do it in part to improve the lot of racially and culturally deserving Arabs and help them rejoin their rightful place in civilized nations.

Le Bon, working for the French government, was trying to win Muslim Arabs under Turkish rule over to France. The way to do it was to belittle the Turkish character and portray Muslim Arabs under a very flattering light with statements such as "Pre-Islamic civilization was not inferior to that of Babylonia." He claimed that to have been able to create a new and brilliant civilization was proof that Arabs had a long history of culture and "aptitudes" preceding Islam.

He then claimed that Muslim Arabs were "the only conquerors in history who allowed the conquered people to practice their faith in complete liberty," forgetting that such freedom was paid for in the form of jizya and therefore tolerance was not a conviction but rather a good to be traded for silver and gold. The alternative was the sword.

He elsewhere states that "Islam was, for all submitted under its law, like Pax Romana" and that "in contact with Arabs, great nations such as Egypt and India adopted their beliefs, customs, and even their architecture."

Lawrence of Arabia did the same for Britain three decades later by helping the "brave and superior" Bedouins with their surplus British rifles and camels overthrow their Turkish oppressors and take Damascus, just like their ancestors did in 634.

In addition to reframing Arab history to suit their own purposes, Europeans repeated stories relayed by Ottoman and Mameluke writers, who, in turn, relayed stories written by chroniclers from the Abbasid period, who aggrandized Arab historical prowess in an attempt to compete with the ascending Persians.

Upon reading Le Bon and other similar orientalists such as Ernest Renan, Muslim Arab nationalists started to repeat what they read until it became unquestioned truth. Such truth made it into school textbooks and radio programs (such as the wildly popular radio saga of pre-Islamic Arab hero Sayf Ibn Yazan) and created proud generations of Arabs ready to reestablish their glorious past.

The third attempt was made by twentieth-century Muslims mostly after independence to create a mythologized history as part of nation building. A good example are the writings of Agha Ibrahim Akram (1923–1989), a Pakistani general who wrote several "history" books about early Muslim conquests. He wrote a glorious biography (*The Sword of Allah*, published in Karachi in 1970) for Khālid ibn al-Walīd, the famous general who presumably defeated both the armies of Sasanian Persia and the Byzantine Empire. He relied heavily on medieval writings and made no attempt to verify or test any statements previously made. His objective was to provide the newly formed Pakistan and its army, in the throes of an ongoing conflict with India, with an uplifting book extolling the intrinsic invincibility of Islam. It is unfortunate that these inaccuracies are perpetuated by the likes of Wikipedia, which relied heavily on this book in drafting its page dedicated to Khālid ibn al-Walīd.

Such manufactured pride understandably morphed into hatred of the West after the utter failure of the policies of Muslim countries by the close of the '70s in the form of socialist nationalism in Egypt, Iraq, Syria, and Algeria and neo-colonial liberalism in Morocco, Saudi Arabia, and Jordan. The ensuing growing resentment of the West naturally helped Islamists to expand their base starting in the '80s.

The perceived attack of the West on Islam was reinforced by the advent of a revisionist school of Islamic studies which challenged a great deal of the inherited dogma. Members of this school argued that the Islamic historical tradition had been greatly corrupted in transmission. They tried to correct or reconstruct the early history of Islam from other, presumably more reliable, sources—such as inscriptions on coins, stones, and early Christian sources. John Wansbrough (1928–2002) initiated this movement, and his deep, and oftentimes unwarranted, skepticism influenced a number of other scholars, such as Patricia Crone (1945–2015) and Michael Cook (1940–).

In 1977, Crone and Cook published *Hagarism: The Making of the Islamic World*, which argued that the traditional early history of Islam is a myth, generated *after* the Arab conquests of Egypt, Syria, and Persia to prop up the new Arab regimes in those countries. Using scattered and incomplete early Christian sources, they suggested that the Qur'an was composed after Muhammad's death and that the Arab conquests may have been the *cause*, rather than the *consequence*, of Islam.

The de-emphasis of Abbasid histories and the focus on contemporary Christian sources such as Sebeos, John of Nikiû, Theophanes, Theophilus of Edessa, and others gained more ascendency.

Tom Holland, in his book *In the Shadow of the Sword*, recaps some of Patricia Crone's ideas in his typical flamboyant way. He narrates a full deconstructionist interpretation of nascent Islam that denies the existence of pre-Islamic Mecca, tries to divide the Prophet Muhammad into two characters (along the obvious fault line of the different tone of the revelations from Mecca and Medina), and imagines early Islam as a Jewish-Christian heresy aspiring to conquer the Holy Land. Revisionists also tend to cite non-Muslim sources in preference to anything that can be seen to have been composed in Abbasid Baghdad.

Robert Hoyland, in his book *In God's Path*, is less speculative and more subdued but acknowledges that the conquests were Arabic, not Muslim, in nature, and that the contributions of Arab Christians were grossly understated.

Revisionist Western archeologists joined the new chorus led by the historians. The German scholar Gerd R. Puin, investigating Qur'an fragments from the early eighth century found in an old mosque in Sana'a, Yemen, (known as the Sana'a manuscripts) and noting unconventional verse orderings, minor textual variations, and rare styles of orthography, suggested that some of the parchments were palimpsests in which some text has been scraped and rewritten later on, and jumped to the conclusion that this implied an evolving text as opposed to a fixed one. In other words, most of the Qur'an, just like the Bible, may have been written over time after the Prophet's death.

The issue is that academic research so far has relied on biased sources, both Christian and Muslim, and on underwhelming archaeological evidence. The new focus on Christian sources, while welcome, does not appear to get historians any closer to the truth. Sebeos, the Armenian bishop, wrote about the conquests around 660, more than twenty years after they occurred, and he certainly was not an eyewitness to any of the events he related. His chronicles are based on hearsay and are tainted by his ecclesiastical position and hatred of Muslims. John of Nikiû, the Coptic bishop, wrote his chronicle around 694, sixty years after the events. Theophilus of Edessa wrote detailed accounts of the Yarmuk battle around 760, over a century later. Clearly, and just like Tabari, he made no attempt to verify his accounts and just repeated the stories he had heard. Theophanes wrote a similar mythical account of Yarmuk forty years after Theophilus repeating the same narrative.

Muslim historians such as Tabari (836–923), al-Mas'udi (896–956), Ibn Hisham (died 834), and al-Baladhuri (died 892) wrote even later, had a very clear Muslim bias, and wrote even taller tales.

Coin inscriptions, incomplete scrolls, and other limited archaeological artifacts cannot, alone, be the basis for far-reaching conclusions rejecting major historical events.

Proposed Methodology

My own methodology will acknowledge but not overly rely on either Muslim or Christian sources or incomplete archaeological evidence. Acknowledging these unreliable sources, whether Muslim or Christian, does not mean that we should surrender, or put a hold on, our critical abilities and common sense.

Instead, I give more weight to facts on the ground at the time the events occurred, such as demographics, economics, social norms, topography, and impact all of these factors normally are expected to have on the course of events. I then use this information to test events as reported and provide more credence to what fits my understanding of the factual background and less credence to what does not.

As an example, I will analyze the demographics, war history, and social structure of the peninsular Arabs to determine whether Arabia had the manpower and other prerequisites to levy armies, as often mentioned in the old accounts. Also, while all historians focused on peninsular Arabs, very few ever discussed the whereabouts and impact of the Fertile Crescent Christian Arabs who outnumbered peninsular Arabs and had much more military experience and equipment given their military service with the Byzantine and Sasanian Empires.

Therefore, I will study and compare both groups in the few decades before the conquests. I believe that studying the dichotomy between these two arabophobe populations can shed an important light on the course of events in the critical second and third decades of the seventh century.

Another example is the Battle of Yarmuk, which has traditionally been universally viewed as the battle that ended Byzantine presence in Syria. Most accounts state that about 40,000 Arab soldiers defeated 120,000 Byzantine troops. The problem is that the battlefield's terrain is so uneven with so many ravines that there is not enough room for 20,000 troops to camp, let alone 160,000! This is not even counting family members who typically accompanied Arab warriors during military operations (wives were the ones providing the food, caring for the wounded, and imparting a moral force to their husbands). In addition, the Yarmuk River, which is a small tributary that empties into the Jordan River, becomes no more than a small stream during the summer months in the arid area of the border between Syria and Jordan. So it is impossible that there was sufficient water (a minimum of a gallon a day per person and two per horse) for 160,000 troops and approximately fifty thousand horses during six days of fighting in the middle of the month of August!

My methodology, in a nutshell, is to provide the reader with a factual assessment of the demographic, social, and economic background along with a view of the complexity of the situation and preponderance of the evidence and probable course of events and cast him in the role of the historian, allowing him to evaluate probabilities and reach conclusions based on a rational interpretation of information.

I will, therefore, dedicate the first two chapters of this book to the factual comparison of peninsular pagan Arabs and Fertile Crescent Christian Arabs along demographic, social, and economic dimensions. This analysis shows that Arabs prior to Islam were not a monolithic population and that a clear dichotomy can be established between the peninsular and Fertile Crescent Arabs. This dichotomy will be very helpful in understanding the events that occurred after the end of the Byzantine-Sasanian War in 628.

The following table recaps the primary differences between the peninsular pagan Arabs and Fertile Crescent Christian Arabs:

Dimension	Peninsular Arabs	Fertile Crescent Arabs
Political structure	Not centralized	Centralized
Population around 628	150,000	700,000
Military experience	Very little; not warlike	Extensive
Religion	Mostly pagan	Mostly Christian
Lifestyle	About 80% nomads	About 80% sedentary
Occupation	Mostly pastoralists	Mostly soldiers and farmers

Chapter 3 will use the conclusions reached in the prior two chapters to chart the most probable course of events considering known facts and comparing such probable course to the historical course as reported by sources.

This is a modest attempt in reassessing an important moment in Islamic history based on forensic analysis of the facts and circumstances surrounding events. Unlike prior accounts which were pre-ordained and served to buttress an ideology and comply with a dogma, I let my findings lead to whatever conclusions with no pre-conceptions. I believe that Arabs, including myself, are comfortable enough with their identity to try to attempt to remove falsehoods from their historical records, so they can establish a more likely and balanced picture of their past and, in so doing, illuminate the path to a better future.

CHAPTER ONE

Peninsular Arabs

Topography and Climate

The Arabian Peninsula is the largest peninsula in the world at 1.25 million square miles and consists of the current countries of Saudi Arabia, Yemen, Oman, Qatar, Bahrain, Kuwait, and the United Arab Emirates. It is bordered by the Red Sea to the west and southwest, the Persian Gulf to the northeast, Syria and Iraq to the north, and the Indian Ocean to the southeast.

The southwest (Yemen) consists of a well-watered mountain country which from an early date permitted the rise of agriculture and the development of relatively advanced sedentary civilizations. The remainder of the peninsula consists of waterless steppes and deserts broken only by an occasional oasis and crossed by a few caravan routes. The population was mainly pastoral and nomadic, living by its flocks of camels and goats and by raiding the peoples of the oases, the cultivated neighboring areas to the north, or each other.

The core of the peninsula (center and north) is traditionally divided into three zones. The first of these is the Tihama, a Semitic word meaning 'lowland," applied to the undulating plains and slopes of the Red Sea coast. The second, moving eastward, is the Hejaz or "barrier." This term was originally applied only to the mountain range separating the coastal plain from the plateau of Najd but was later extended to include much of the coastal plain itself. To the east of the Hejaz lies the great inland plateau of Najd, most of it consisting of rocky desert.

Between these zones communications are limited and difficult, depending mainly on wadis, so that the inhabitants of the different parts of the peninsula had little contact with one another.

The desert climate, which is prevalent in the entire peninsula, apart from pockets in the southwest, is marked by high temperatures during the day and low temperatures at night. This climate did not encourage travel, trade, or agriculture.

There is evidence that human habitation in the Arabian Peninsula dates to about 100,000 to 130,000 years ago. However, the harsh climate historically prevented much settlement in the pre-Islamic Arabian peninsula, excluding Yemen, apart from a small number of urban trading settlements, such as Mecca and Medina (Yathrib), located in the Hejaz in the west of the peninsula.

Organization Based on Tribalism

The dominant feature of the population of Central and Northern Arabia in the period immediately preceding the rise of Islam is Bedouin tribalism.

In Bedouin society the social unit is the group, not the individual. The latter has rights and duties only as a member of his group. The group is held together externally by the need for self-defense against the hardships and dangers of desert life and internally by the blood tie of descent in the male line.

The livelihood of the tribe depends on their herds and on raiding the neighboring settled countries and caravans crossing Arabia.

The political organization of the tribe was rudimentary. Its head was the *sheikh*, an elected leader who was rarely more than a first among equals. He followed rather than led tribal opinion. The sheikh could neither impose duties nor inflict penalties. His function was arbitration rather than command. He was advised by a council of elders typically called the *majlis*, consisting of the heads of the families and representatives of clans within the tribe.

Tribes were divided into clans, which rarely exceeded 150 people. The average tribe was comprised of about a dozen clans. Each clan would have no more than about twenty able-bodied men, owning a handful of iron swords among themselves. The clan chief typically owned a horse.

Generally, clans of a tribe were scattered over large, non-adjacent areas. It is therefore not possible to define a tribe by its territory. This situation also did not allow tribes to muster large numbers of fighters in a reasonable period. This, in turn, made large engagements impossible. Even if communication among clans could occur and assuming most clans followed the call, no tribe could muster more than four hundred fighters of whom only about half would wield iron swords or spears and only a dozen rode horses.

Such aggregation was very rare because peninsular Arab tribes had no common effective leadership and rarely united for any common activities. As a matter of fact, political division and dissension within a tribe was the rule rather than the exception. Whenever sources reported a joint tribal activity, it often turned out that the report was false.

Here and there settled nomads established small towns in oases. The most important of these were Mecca, Ta'if, and Yathrib in the Hejaz. The number of towns was, however, very small and never exceeded a handful in the Hejaz and Najd.

Tribes emphasized lineage and took pride in it. This fostered a deep sense of pride, as each tribe viewed itself as more noble and superior than the others. Such feeling substantially survived the advent of Islam. Tribal prejudice, lack of discipline, and inability to consistently accept command were never conducive to the creation of cohesive military bodies. During the conquests, each tribe had its own battalion and gave allegiance to its own military chief, not to the supreme commander selected by the caliph.

Temperament

Contrary to what longstanding popular sagas suggest, peninsular Arabs were not warlike people. As a rule, they avoided fighting and always sought settlements. When fighting broke out, it typically lasted a few hours and resulted in no or very little bloodshed. We will illustrate this point later.

When not taking care of their camels, Bedouins kept an eye out for plunder or just causing damage. They would plunder whatever they were able to lay their hands on without having to fight or expose themselves to danger. If an oasis stronghold appeared difficult to attack, they would bypass it in favor of easier prey.

In addition to not being warlike, peninsular Arabs were not particularly religious either. Their conformity with religious practice followed tribal inertia and was dictated by their conservative respect for tradition. Nowhere do we find an illustration of genuine devotion to a pagan god. Unlike the Greek, Roman, or Persian worlds, Arabia had no temples or sacred sanctuaries to speak of, other than in Mecca and Ta'if.

Rather, the Bedouin worshipped local sacred rocks and demons called *jinn*. These jinn differ from the gods not so much in their nature as in their relation to man. The gods are friendly overall; the jinn hostile—personifications of the fantastic notions of the terrors of the desert and its wild animal life. Even after Islam the idea of the jinn persisted; indeed, the number of jinn increased, since the pagan gods were then degraded (but not forgotten) into jinn.

This is to say that peninsular Arabs were not special among ethnic groups in being overly moved by devotion or faith. Being practical people (as the desert requires), what moves them more is the excitement of raids and plunder. It was not religious zeal that got unmarried poor Bedouin young men (who outnumbered available young Arab women by a ratio of two to one as we shall see) to join the conquests, but rather their normal lust for sex and plunder added to the wonder of seeing more hospitable lands. Given the expected benefits, most of them were certainly unwilling to sacrifice themselves in the name of any faith.

Demographics

At the time of the Prophet, the entire population of the Arabian Peninsula could not have exceeded 150,000 people as Ibn Khaldun states in his Muqaddimah. This number excludes approximately 20,000 Jews who lived mostly in Northwestern Arabia (Yathrib and Khaybar for the most part) and thousands of Ethiopians who lived in South Arabia and Hejaz.

Therefore, population density was minuscule: about less than one person per eight square miles. Arabs lived in small clans and moved constantly, and therefore, it was common for a clan not to encounter another in over a matter of months. This situation was not conducive to disputes since the area was huge, number of oases large, population very small, and encounters rare. This situation also naturally promoted consanguinity as I will discuss later.

In addition, widespread female infanticide kept the birth rate depressed. Female infanticide was due to a variety of factors: removal of babies with physical abnormalities and sick infants, elimination of social illegitimates, reactions to the loss of the mother during childbirth, manipulation of sex ratio, and, last but not least, possible prevention of loss of honor. This is because a significant percentage of brides was acquired through kidnapping.

In Arab pre-Islamic tradition (sunna), killing a newborn by burying it alive with no bloodshed was considered humane and hence not murder. The father would simply dig a hole next to the mother, and when she gave birth to an unwanted female child, although on occasion it might also be a male child, the newborn was directly buried in the hole.

Infanticide was also a means for the prevention of poverty and considered to be an acceptable solution for the liability of a female child. Males were considered stronger and useful, while females were considered an economic burden, especially during times of famine. The father's disappointment and fear of the female being held captive by an opposing tribe which would bring shame to the clan was an important factor.

Consanguinity Created a Weaker Than Average Population

Tribalism gave each tribe a sense of pride in its lineage and superiority over others. This promoted tribal inter-marriages, especially between cousins. The rate was a staggering 80 percent. Such inbreeding caused alarming rates of hereditary diseases. Some disorders were many times more common in Arabia compared to the Byzantine and Sasanian Empires. There are still tribes in Saudi Arabia today that have distinctive malformations due to consanguinity that are recognizable from their appearance.

The weakened gene pool made peninsular Arabs sick. The majority of those born with metabolic diseases, severe malformations, and blood disorders would die soon after birth or never reach reproductive age. Many of the survivors suffered from varying degrees of intellectual disability and hereditary diseases that significantly lessened the quality and duration of their lives.

As stated earlier, the low status of females and their perception as honor destroyers promoted female infanticide to the point where the ratio male to female was approximately two to one. As a result, many men could not find a bride and resorted to an accepted form of marriage where several men shared a single woman, and in the case of birth, the woman had the exclusive right of assigning fatherhood to one of the men. The selected man was obligated to accept such assignment.

The birth rate was low (due to the lack of births and high rate of infant mortality), and the population was, therefore, stable over a period of several centuries. The life expectancy was low: eliminating individuals who died before adulthood, the mean life expectancy for women was about forty years; for men, it was approximately forty-five years. Men lived longer simply because they worked less, and as we will see later, there was very little warfare to diminish their numbers.

Out of the approximate population of 150,000, two-thirds were men. Only about a quarter of the 100,000 were able-bodied, between the ages of eighteen and thirty-fie, and fit for sustained military service, i.e., no more than 25,000. If one out of every two able-bodied men joined the Rashidun army, that would be 13,000, which is the agreed upon number of the Rashidun army immediately after the death of Muhammad in 632.

Contrast the total peninsular Arab population of about 150,000 to the population of the Byzantine Empire of 17 million (of whom 400,000 were Ghassanid Christian Arabs) and the Sasanian Empire of 10 million (of whom 300,000 were Lakhmid Christian Arabs). That is a combined 27 million versus 150,000.

Lack of Common Identity

The geography of Arabia made the construction of large political entities or an ethnos very difficult. Clans, even the ones belonging to the same tribe, had very little chance to encounter each other in the vastness of Arabia. As a result, tribal cohesion was not strong. Furthermore, an Arab common identity did not exist prior to the conquests.

A common identity began to take shape once these peoples came together under the banner of Islam and coalesced for the first time in the *amṣar*, the Arab tent garrisons created in Iraq (such as Kufa) and Egypt. Each *miṣr* (singular of amṣar) counted between three and five thousand warriors and was enough to remotely control two to three million peaceful, unarmed individuals. The exception was Syria where the Ghassanids had effective military control and therefore there was no need for a peninsular Arab miṣr.

For the first time, and over a period of a couple of generations (between 640 and 690), these people created a common language and started to imagine a "national history." The creation of this identity accelerated during Abbasid times to counteract a rising Persian influence and its associated Persian pre-Islamic civilization and imperial narrative. The creation of a pre-Islamic Arab national identity with its heroes and poetry was largely the invention of an urban Iraqi imagination threatened by the rise of Persian influence under Abbasid rule.

Nostalgia to an imagined earlier freedom also pushed urban Iraqis to create the image of a free, powerful, and flamboyant Arab Bedouin displaying generosity, eloquence, and freedom that no urbanites, in any time, can enjoy. Later Abbasid writers wanted to believe that the Arab Bedouin stereotype reflected Islam's past. At a time when Arabs were pushed aside by Persians and Turks starting in the mid-ninth century, the creation of the pre-Islamic hero allowed them to conceptualize the miraculous birth of the Islamic empire from a pagan desert void and, in doing so, bestowed a sense of mythical wonderment to the past. It also allowed them to conceptualize a superior civilization when compared to the Persian civilization that preceded them.

There was also a revived interest in the pre-Islamic *war ayyam* (war days) of the Arabs. Writings multiplied during the Abbasid period as a debate raged between Persians and Arabs about which group had a superior culture and civilization. The constant recounting and embellishment of the ayyam served to bolster Arab pride in front of the Persian and Turkish onslaught. No wonder such stories came to convert simple skirmishes into full-blown battles, and full-blown pre-Islamic poems never heard of before suddenly appeared.

In short, a well-defined Arab identity did not exist until the Abbasid period and was created in large part to counteract Persian ascendency.

So the question is the following: if an Arab common identity and unity did not exist and could not have fueled the success of the Arab conquests, what did? If peninsular Arabs did not have the required numbers or strength, who helped them wage those wars?

Lack of Central Government or Standing Army

The Arabian Peninsula, excluding Yemen and the northwestern part of the peninsula (traditionally under Byzantine foederati rule), never experienced a central authority above that of the tribe. In addition, kingship had a different meaning: Yemeni tribes viewed the king as no more than an arbiter. The Yemeni king's title was *muqarrib* ("mediator" in Arabic). His job was limited to reconciling the points of view of the various tribes and mediating in case of conflict. His power could not be compared to that of Roman or Persian emperors or even to that of the negus in Ethiopia. At any rate, whatever semblance of kingdoms there was in Yemen, they all had collapsed by 525, the start date of the Ethiopian Aksumite occupation, which was followed in 570 by Persian occupation through 628.

By the birth of Mohammad in 570, Arab "kingdoms" were long gone. Tribes were divided into clans named after an ancestor and were governed by a sheikh. The clan was the primary political structure.

This meant that a central government never developed to check the centrifugal power of the tribes. The advent of Islam did not weaken the power of the tribe. It encouraged it. Islam made full use of the tribal system for its military and colonization purposes. It divided the army into units based on tribal lines, settled the colonists in the conquered lands in tribes, and treated new converts from among the subjugated peoples as "clients" (mawali) of such tribes. By a "client," Arabs ordinarily mean one who seeks voluntarily to become a member of a chosen tribe. The tribal spirit was never outgrown by the Arab character as it developed after the rise of Islam and was among the determining factors that led to the disintegration and ultimate downfall of the various Islamic states.

Lack of Trade Among Tribes and Absence of Local Currency

Tribes raided each other and had very little to offer to each other or trade. Tribesmen purchased supplies from towns and oases. But they preferred to steal supplies instead of purchasing or bartering.

Because the economy was largely based on auto-sufficiency, bartering, and raiding, Arabs never developed their own currency (except for copies made primarily of Greek tetradrachms in Yemen and Nabatea). These coins were used for large transactions or tax payment only. The great majority of everyday transactions were cashless. Arab merchants in Mecca made extensive use of the Byzantine gold solidus and Persian silver drachm for large and medium-sized transactions, respectively, and the Byzantine copper 40-*nummi* follis (known in Arabic as *fels*) for smaller everyday transactions. Meccan and Yathribi merchants used gold *solidi* for their transactions with the Ghassanids and Byzantine Syrians and silver drachms in transactions with the Lakhmids and Sasanian Persians. The bulk of trade was with Syria.

The Byzantine 40-*nummi* follis was the coin of choice used by Arabs prior to and during the days of Muhammad, and it is the coin he would have handled the most. The great majority of sedentary Arabs never owned a gold coin.

Nomads, on the other hand, rarely saw a coin. Merchant caravan escorters, such as the Ghassanids, occasionally paid tolls to tribes in follis or fels, prior to crossing their territories, to create goodwill and avoid unnecessary skirmishes. This allowed sheikhs to distribute a portion of the toll to the more important tribe members. This was the only currency the Bedouins had access to, and they used it to buy necessities at town markets.

Very Short, Low-Intensity Warfare

Peninsular Arabs were not warlike people because they did not need to be. The peninsula is huge, and their numbers were so few that it was rare for two clans to bump into each other and fight over a well or an oasis.

Unlike sedentary societies (such as the Byzantine or Sasanian) where farmers invested so much in their fields that they felt the need to protect their holdings (crops, granaries, tools, and belongings), sometimes to the death (not doing so would most likely mean starvation), nomadic Arab Bedouins, by contrast, had nothing to protect or die for. When a weaker clan encountered a stronger one vying for the same resource, the weaker clan typically gave the stronger one a wide berth and kept looking for another well. Sedentary people always had less room for compromise than nomads did and therefore were better prepared for fighting than nomads because they needed to be.

In addition, and over time, it became widely known and accepted (Arab sunna) that certain tribes had the right of first use of certain wells and oases, and so the other clan when seeing that the owners of first right of use were present, just moved on.

When clans or tribes fought each other, the bulk of military activity was based on individuals championing their tribes, or clans engaging in single combat. Melees were rare, and formation combat unheard of. Arabs were not familiar with military concepts such as flanks, avant-garde, rear guard, reserves, or anything close to that. When on rare occasions melee fights broke out, they consisted of a confused crowd of young men, and sometimes women, hitting each other with stones, sticks, palm fronds, and occasionally daggers and iron swords.

The bulk of the fighting occurred primarily because of the kidnapping of women. This was driven by the general unavailability of women as a consequence of widespread female infanticide. The great majority of fights consisted of raids that lasted a few hours, certainly less than a day. Arabs were utterly unfamiliar with the concept of campaigns that lasted for more than a day. This had an impact on logistics during the conquests: warriors were expected to provide their own food. And since men did not carry much food with them (just enough for two or three days) because surplus was unavailable, they ended up living off the land as they went. But as most of the terrain they crossed was barren, they often went hungry. There was also no supply train. Men carried their tents and supplies. Many had none. Of course, there was no medical care of any sort.

Camels represented 99 percent of all mounts. But not everyone owned one. Most warriors walked barefoot. The horse, unlike the camel, was an animal of luxury whose feeding and care constituted a great challenge to the man of the desert. Its possession was a presumption of wealth and typically confined to the sheikh and rich high born. There were only a few hundred horses in all of peninsular Arabia.

Given the above, pre-Islamic warfare in peninsular Arabia was very uncommon, and when it occurred consisted of very short bloodless skirmishes.

But before discussing the most famous peninsular battles preceding Islam, it would be helpful first to describe what Arab warriors had at hand to fight with.

Lack of Weaponry

Warriors were expected to provide their own weapons. This was also true of warriors who joined the conquest campaigns in the 630s.

The principal weapon was the short-blade iron sword, not the curved scimitar of popular imagination. Even such a rudimentary weapon was expensive and therefore scarce. The best swords made of steel were mostly imported from India (a few were made in Yemen using imported Indian steel) and were very rare and expensive. Steel swords were so precious that they were given names and handed down in families. Most of them were decades old and not properly maintained. There were no more than a few dozen in the entire peninsula.

Spears, both the long (*rumh*) and short (*harba*) types were not widely used. Arab bows were much simpler than their Persian or Byzantine counterparts and had a much shorter range (less than 150 yards). The weapons used by most warriors were thick sticks and stones. Chain mail body armor was extremely rare. Only one man out of five hundred would have it. Head protection was non-existent. The few horses used had no saddles and no stirrups (first stirrups were used in central Asia at the start of the eighth century) which made horses not maneuverable in close combat. Camels, much more available, were a real liability in close combat. As a result, and contrary to heroic events related in poems, most of the fighting was done on foot. The poems never mentioned the use of any sort of siege engines, as Arabs never needed them (the few towns that existed were not walled) and therefore never built or acquired any.

In conclusion, it is fair to say that Muslims had no secret weapons and no mastery of new military technology with which to offset their low headcount, and as I mentioned earlier, the nomad's mentality tends to be less warlike than that of sedentary farmers, as they have fewer vital possessions to protect.

Now, some will say, what about the famous wars of Dahis and Ghabra, Basus, Fijar, and Sumair which were extensively documented and sung in word and verse over the centuries? And why call *skirmishes* wars at all? In fact, Arabs called any fighting which extended for more than a day (*yawm*), even if such days (*ayyam*) were not consecutive, a war. Even if it was bloodless.

Let's then describe some of the more popular of these so-called Pre-Islamic peninsular wars.

The Dahis and Ghabra "War"

Indeed such "war" lasted for forty years. It started because two tribes, the 'Abs and Dhubyan, placed bets on two camels during a race. As was to be expected, the two tribes contested the outcome of the race. The so-called war took its name from the names of the two racing camels. Contesting the outcome of bets was very common and often resulted in violence. The bad news in this particular case is that the 'Abs counted Antara ibn Shaddad as one of its members, and he singlehandedly accounted for more than half of the casualties.

However, this "war" consisted of only four days of fighting in which nine men were killed, in addition to nine hostage children who were murdered at some point in a fit of rage when the two parties would not agree on a settlement. This meant that there was, on average, one fight every ten years. Fighting casualties were about one man every four years.

These facts did not stop Arab writers, at the start of the crusades four hundred years later, to elevate Antara to the status of a demi-god and attribute thousands of deaths to this Arab Hercules.

The Basus "War"

The Basus "War" also lasted about forty years, but it only consisted of five days of fighting in which a total of twelve men were killed. As with all fighting, it occurred on foot with most fighters being barefoot and yielding sticks or stones. It started because a man named Kulayb of the tribe of Taghlib was killed by a member of the tribe of Bakr. The problem was that the deceased's brother, a drunk poet named Abu Layla ibn Rabi'a (but answering to al-Muhalhil), was a deranged man who dedicated the rest of his life to taking revenge. Three or four of the dead Bakr were killed by al-Muhalhil in single combat.

The Fejar "War"

This is the only known conflict which involved Mecca since its founding. It lasted four years but consisted of only eight days of fighting. The prophet, while a young man, was apparently involved in at least one day of fighting. Because of Muhammad's involvement, many stories were written over time to describe the ferocity of the fighting and the courage displayed by the prophet. No number of casualties was given by any chronicler. However, they all agreed that the difference in casualties between the two sides (Quraysh and Kinanah vs. Qays ʿAylān) was twenty. The confusion and the low difference in casualties count prove that this "war" was no more ferocious than Basus or Dahis and Ghabra.

The Sumair "War"

This conflict occurred between the Aws and the Khazraj, the two largest Arab tribes in and around Yathrib. It lasted for about twenty years and resulted in one death, the same death that sparked the "war"! The rest of the casualties were light wounds inflicted by stones or sticks. As good thick sticks or staffs were a rare commodity, most of the fighters, which included women, used palm fronds. It should be noted that the two tribes were both Azdi from Yemen (just like the Ghassanids) and most likely never meant to inflict much damage on each other, notwithstanding Arab vendetta traditions.

The Buʾath "War"

It is unclear what sparked this conflict between the Aws and the Khazraj. But the Jews of Yathrib interceded and, at some point, gave several Jewish boys as hostages to the Khazraj. The fighting consisted of a single day, even though preparation for it lasted several years. It resulted in two dead from the Aws and one from the Khazraj. That single day of fighting was sparked by the Khazraj massacring the Jewish boys.

Many of these "wars" lasted forty years because, according to tribal tradition, a blood feud could not go on longer than forty years. The blood feuds between the Aws and Khazraj in Yathrib were particularly taxing because, unlike the expansive desert where tribes in conflict lived far enough from each other to avoid most contact when engaged in a blood feud, in the close quarters of Yathrib where both the Aws and Khazraj shared the same water sources, markets, and streets, one was constantly bumping into members of the other tribe. This explains why Yathribi residents were so keen on recruiting the help of Muhammad as an arbiter.

Muslim Faith Was Tempered by the Tenacity of Paganism

Some Muslim chroniclers acknowledged the low peninsular Arab headcount and their lack of military acumen and equipment and so invoked a new and fierce faith as an offsetting factor. Let's discuss the state of this new faith as experienced by Arabs.

Just like other populations that converted from paganism to a monotheist faith before them, Arabs were religiously conservative, and it took them generations to overcome long-held beliefs.

In the case of Christianity, for nearly a hundred years after the conversion of Emperor Constantine, the following Roman emperors denounced the practice of paganism with very little results. In the last years of the Western Roman Empire, the diviners of Africa were still practicing their arts among the nominal Christians of Aquitaine. Long after the external rites of paganism had been suppressed in Italy and elsewhere, the pagan tone and spirit retained its hold on men's imagination. This hold was so powerful and so enduring that the church carried on the tradition of pagan Rome. The cycle of the Christian year was, in many points, adapted to the pagan calendar. The cult of saints and martyrs was established at the very altars where incense had been offered to Mars or Bacchus.

At Naples, lamps burning before the image of the Virgin took the place of those before the family gods. Inscriptions from the fourth and fifth century reveal the enduring power of the worship of Isis, of the Great Mother and Mithra.

In short, in that age, as in our own, there were widely different conceptions of the meaning of the Christian faith. There can be little doubt that there was a vast mass of interested and perfunctory conformity to the religion which had become the established religion of both the Western and Eastern Roman Empires.

Arab paganism was no exception. Long after the advent of Islam, diviners were practicing their trade among the Muslims; all kinds of sorcerers were invoking jinn, writing talismans, concocting magical potions, interpreting dreams, and reading the future.

Islam did not attempt to remove most of the old idols. The jinn stayed, the sacred black stone in the Kaaba stayed, the old rituals of pilgrimage, including animal sacrifice, stayed.

The continuing belief in jinn under Islam is quite telling: the doctrine of demons is the foundation of the belief in incantations and magic. The demons are also the powers acting as mediators between the gods (before Islam) and Allah (after Islam) and mortal men. Along with certain divine qualities, demons have all the passions of humanity; they are irritated by neglect or soothed by gifts and sacrificial rites. From them comes the knowledge of the future by augury and dreams and the power to command the elements, by occult arts, songs, incantations, and potions.

Islam, by keeping the belief in the jinn intact, did not change any of this. Such weak condemnation of symbols of paganism made sure that early Muslims had as much faith in demonic powers as the pagans had.

Nothing could eradicate the belief held by the great majority of Muslim Arabs that there was lore which could control the operations of nature and compel the future to unveil its secrets.

As a matter of fact, the very beginning of Islam was based on a pagan belief. Arabs worshipped mountains as abodes of God in an otherwise flat desertic environment. Dushara and Hubal were mountain gods. The revelation of the Qur'an to Muhammad in a cave in the Hira mountain told the Meccan pagans that the message came from the mountain or God. Caves were viewed as sacred receptacles within God's body, where someone can worship and enter in almost physical contact with God. The Christian Arab and Aramean monks built their monasteries on mountaintops in the Golan and other mountains in Syria, Palestine, and Jordan.

So the cave revelation is an obvious reference to pagan beliefs which were not found to contradict the new religion.

To make matters worse, unlike Christianity, Islam had no clergy that would educate the people in the ways of the new religion. Since the people were illiterate and could not read the Qur'an, they simply copied others, and so developed a formal and perfunctory conformity to the religion based on local practice and understanding. This encouraged the advent of sects and the split of Islamic orthodoxy (Sunni vs. Shia and the split within Sunni with its four main branches).

In Christianity, the rich are condemned, and soldiers, as shedders of blood, are doomed to eternal torment, and there was no possibility to serve both Christ and Caesar. Furthermore, Christianity encouraged withdrawal from the world in monasteries to serve God.

The Muslims, on the other hand, judged religion by its utility to men. As a result, they did not believe in withdrawal and believed that Islam encouraged them to get rich by grabbing the spoils of the enemy and there was no difference between serving the caliph (the representative of God on earth) and God.

Islam encouraged enrichment by all legal means. And conquest plunder was legal. Receiving jizya from non-Muslims was also legal and helped the constant replenishment of the Muslim treasury and the pockets of the believers.

It should be stressed here that the great majority of the non-Arab converts were waverers and skeptics to whom the new religion was mostly a means of profit, safety, or ambition.

Therefore, it is quite unlikely that Islam brought about a religious fervor that exceeded that experienced by devout Christians in Byzantium or practicing Zoroastrians in Sasanian Persia.

CHAPTER TWO

Fertile Crescent Arabs

The Fertile Crescent comprises today's Syria, Israel, Lebanon, Jordan, and Iraq. Two main Semitic groups traditionally populated these areas: Aramaic/Syriac-speaking and Arabic-speaking.

The great majority of Arabs living in the Fertile Crescent migrated over time from Yemen. First the Nabateans in the fourth and third century BC, then the Tanûkhids in the first century AD, the Salihids in the second century and the Ghassanids in the fourth century. Such migrations were prompted by climate change, the mounting disrepair and occasional failure of dams (including Marib), and the breakdown of the power of the Mukarribs, whose job was to reconcile differences among Yemeni tribes. Culturally speaking, the region was tricultural: Greek, Aramaic, and Arabic.

This chapter will show how much more advanced and numerous the Fertile Crescent Arabs were, compared to the peninsular Arabs. This will remediate the lack of coverage of their culture and contributions during the conquests by the Muslim Arab historians.

Indeed, Muslim ninth-century chronicles are silent with respect to the contributions of the Levant's Christian Arabs and are, on the other hand, rife with triumphalist statements emphasizing the power of non-existing huge Muslim Arab armies suddenly surging out of the sands of Arabia. According to them, Islam was carried at breakneck speed from Mecca across the whole Middle East by peninsular Arabs, who then established unified rule over all the lands of the former Persian Empire and in all the southern and eastern provinces of the Byzantine Empire in only a few short years. Peninsular Arabs are victorious everywhere; non-Arabs everywhere submit, convert, or are killed; and the Islamic government is imposed everywhere.

This chapter will show that the Muslim ninth-century chronicles were wrong about both the composition of the force behind the conquests as well as in regard to the objective of the conquests. In fact, the Arab occupation of Syria and Iraq was the result of a massive uprising of Christian Arabs revolting against empires that treated them as second-class citizens for so long. This uprising occurred at the exact time that the Arabian Peninsula was being unified under Muhammad and could project a force to take advantage of the uprising. The primary objective of the combined peninsular and Fertile Crescent Arabs was not to convert populations to Islam but rather to gain wealth and status through plunder and taxation of such populations.

In short, the rise of Islam and the early conquests were neither the result of some great and sudden faith that provided superhuman strength to peninsular Arabs nor to some instantaneously acquired military knowledge and courage that the peninsular Arabs never had. It was a direct consequence of the insurrection of the Fertile Crescent Arabs whose force and knowledge were channeled by their peninsular kin.

The Ghassanids

Arab presence in the Levant dates to the fourth century BC. The Nabateans, the builders of Petra, established a kingdom in the second century BC that encompassed the whole territory from the Euphrates to the Red Sea. This kingdom was annexed by the Romans in AD 105. Within three generations, the Nabateans were Romanized to a large extent and elements of the old kingdom blended with imperial traditions to create a distinctive Romanized but Arab-speaking culture. The geographical extent of the Roman Arabian Province consisted of the former Nabataean kingdom in Jordan, southern Syria, southern Palestine, and northwest Saudi Arabia. The inhabitants of these territories were both settled and nomadic Arabs and were citizens of the Byzantine Empire. Nabateans acted as frontier watchmen for the Byzantine Empire policing the border with Arabia and helping against Sasanian incursions. The Nabateans were also active traders who helped move goods from the East into the Roman Empire. They were able to develop a very sophisticated banking and commercial network that covered the entire Roman and Sasanian Empires. Some Nabateans became very wealthy and played a significant role in Roman politics. Two emperors, Elagabalus (r. 218–222) and Philip the Arab (r. 244–249) were partially Nabatean.

The Nabateans were replaced by the Tanûkhids in this role in the fourth century, the Salihids in the fifth century, and finally the Ghassanids in the early sixth century. All these Arab groups had come from South Arabia over time and became Monophysite Christians by the fifth century. They were also mostly sedentary. The Nabatean capital was at Petra, and the Ghassanids' capital was at Jabiya, in the Golan foothills in Syria. Both were quite extensive and accommodated over ten thousand inhabitants each. By the start of the seventh century, the Levantine Arab populations amounted to approximately four hundred thousand.

Christianization

With the conversion of the Roman emperor Constantine to Christianity, the new faith of the Byzantine Empire was at last free to pursue, now with imperial approval and support, its aggressive missionary way not only within but far beyond the frontiers of the empire. The eastern side of the Red Sea became Christian, and then Yemen, and Christianity also spread among the Arab tribes in the northwestern (Ghassanids) and northeastern (Lakhmids) marshes of Arabia.

The Ghassanids were devout Christians who built a multitude of churches and monasteries. The letter of the Monophysite Archimandrites gives the impressive number of 137 Ghassanid monasteries by 570. The Golan, as a holy mountain, was an important monastic region. Mountains, especially mountaintops, attracted monks and hermits and so became, with deserts, the traditional abodes of monks. These monasteries were frequently visited by Christian Arab soldiers who would spend time there learning religious precepts, receiving blessings, and helping monks with daily chores. In return, monks frequently followed these soldiers in their military campaigns to provide moral support, medical help, and last rites.

In the fifth century, the major Arab figure in monasticism was the Salihid king Dāwud (David), who renounced the world. He became a monk and built the famous Dayr Dawud. Another Arab king in the same century, the Lakhmid king Nu'man of Hira, adopted Christianity and became an itinerant monk.

Monasticism spread in Western Arabia and in Tabuk and Hejaz in the sixth century. There were many monasteries such as Dayr Hisma, Dayr Damdam, Dayr al-Qunfud, Wadi al-Qura (outside of Yathrib) and Masajid Maryam (Mary's shrines, not far from Mecca).

Muslim tradition maintains that Muhammad, while working as a caravan leader in the 590s, met the monk Bahira at Dayr Busra (a Ghassanid monastery) outside of the city of Bostra, the terminus of the Via Odorifera used by the Meccans. The influence of the Ghassanids on the prophet during his pre-prophetic period appears to be quite likely.

The monks were the athletes of the spirit—counterparts of the soldiers, the athletes of the body. Thus they became the moral force behind the Ghassanid Christian army guarding the Byzantine limitrophe.

It should be noted that Muslims copied this practice first in the east where communities of *zuhd* (ascetics) sprung up all over Syria, Iraq, and Northern Arabia in the second half of the seventh century and then in the west, particularly in Morocco, where the Murabitun (the Ribat dwellers) created a network of Ribat in the eleventh century where ascetics and soldiers lived together to propagate the word of God (or at least their conservative version of it) both by word and sword. Ribat is a fort specially built to house a light cavalry unit. The capital of Morocco, Rabat, started as one of these monastic strongholds.

Just like the Murabitun, the first Berber Moroccan dynasty which took over the southern half of Iberia after the demise of the Umayyads, each Ghassanid soldier chose or was assigned a monastery, where he would spend some time before a military campaign and then head out to the rallying point with the monks.

Therefore, the Ghassanid fortified monastery, in which soldier and monk lived together, anticipated and foreshadowed the later Muslim Ribat. This situation shows the closeness of monks and soldiers and becomes an important point later.

Centralization and Militarization

As a corollary to Christianization, the Byzantines also realized that the Arabs of the marshes could be of some military use to the empire. In the course of the three centuries that preceded the rise of Islam and the Arab conquests, the Byzantine Empire availed itself of the military services of three Arab groups in succession: the Tanûkhids in the fourth century, the Salihids in the fifth, and the Ghassanids in the sixth century.

These Arab groups were Byzantine allies or foederati who received the Annona (food allotment) and annual stipends in gold and were settled within the Byzantine Diocese of Oriens (the Levant). One of the principal duties of the Arab foederati was the protection of the Byzantine frontier from the inroads of the nomads. Another important duty was participation in the wars against Sasanian Persia and its Arab vassals, the Lakhmids of Hira. This was especially true during the long fifty-year reign of the Lakhmid king Mundir (r. 504–554), who terrorized Syria with his brutality and anti-Christian animosity. But he met his match in the Ghassanid king al-Harith (Aretas) ibn Jabalah (r. 528–569), who killed him in the battle of Chalcis in 554.

In the sixth century, the Ghassanids, in their capacity as foederati, performed an even more vital function. Indeed, al-Harith ibn Jabalah, who was made archphylarch and titled king by Justinian in 529, commanded Byzantine troops in the Persian campaign of 541. It should also be mentioned that, after the Persian War of 540–545, Justinian disbanded the Byzantine frontier guard corps (*limitanei*) and transferred their duties along with their frontier forts to the Ghassanids. At that point, al-Harith added the title of *limitaneus* to those of *archphylarch* and *basileus* (king). By the end of Justinian's reign in 565, the Ghassanids were the primary military force in charge of protecting the entire Levant.

They were indeed a major military force to be reckoned with. The Ghassanid light armored cavalry had no match except for certain Sasanian and Lakhmid cavalry units. Indeed, the Ghassanid cavalry consistently outperformed the Byzantine cavalry.

To better appreciate the pivotal place of the Ghassanids in the Byzantine defense system, one has to consider that, unlike Byzantine's other allies who were defending the Western Roman Empire along the Danube and the Rhine and were facing barbarians such as the Germans, Huns, and Sarmatians, the Ghassanids, as the primary contingent in the army of the Orient, were facing a world power: Sasanian Persia.

They, therefore, bore the major brunt of the defense of the Christian Holy Land because they were stationed in the three provinces that surrounded it, the Provincia Arabia, Palaestina Secunda, and Palaestina Tertia.

The Ghassanids were not only soldiers fighting the wars of Byzantium but also agents for peace as patrons of the Monophysite church and of Arabic poetry for which their court at Jabiya became the destination of poets from all over the Arabian Peninsula. Their architectural achievements were not limited to the construction or renovations of forts and fortresses. They built palaces, mansions, churches, monasteries, and audience halls. Jabiya, their capital, was so large and well-endowed that Mu'āwiyah, the founder of the Umayyad dynasty, made it his capital while he was governor of Syria between 640 and 660. Mu'āwiyah also availed himself of the skills and expertise of the Ghassanids in running the new caliphate.

Jabiya

A concise description of Jabiya is worthwhile in order to demonstrate the sedentary nature of Ghassanid society and the sophistication of its culture. As stated earlier, Mu'āwiyah used it as his capital for about twenty years while he was governor of Syria. This indicates that Jabiya had all the necessary facilities and amenities to support a court. Even after the move of the capital from Jabiya to Damascus when Mu'āwiyah became caliph, it continued to be of pivotal importance to the Umayyads for the next hundred years. It also remained the principal military camp of Syria until the reign of Caliph Sulayman.

Just as Jabiya was the cradle of the Sufyānid branch where Mu'āwiyah established the power of his house, so it became for the Marwanid branch in 685, when power was transferred to it under Marwan ibn al-Hakam. It was at Jabiya that he unfurled his banner before he marched to win the battle of Marj Rahit.

The fact that Mu'āwiyah chose to use Jabiya as his capital, instead of any other city in Syria, shows that he trusted and relied on the Ghassanids to a significant extent. This point needs to be remembered, as it becomes an important point later.

It should also be noted that the Battle of Yarmuk (636) is sometimes referred to as the battle of Jabiya because the site of the battle is only a few miles from the city. It becomes clear that the Byzantine army was targeting Jabiya. The reason for such targeting will also become clearer later.

Commerce

The Ghassanids also promoted and protected trade. As such, they oversaw the policing of a segment of the Via Odorifera, running from Tabuk in Northwestern Arabia to Bostra, and a segment of the Strata Diocletiana extending from Bostra to Sura on the Euphrates. They were also entrusted with collecting taxes at the fairs and at certain points along the routes as well as with the task of pursuing and arresting tax dodging merchants.

The outbreak of the Persian Wars at the start of the sixth century, and continuing hostilities in the reign of every emperor until Heraclius, diverted commerce from the Mesopotamian route (along the Euphrates river and then west to Antioch) to the West Arabian route (from Yemen, through Mecca and ending in Bostra), resulting in a profitable caravan trade that enriched both Ghassanids and Meccans, at least until the takeover of Yemen by Persia in 570.

Another reason for the decline in activity of the Mesopotamian route was that the most important commodity carried over the Mesopotamian route was silk. In the mid-sixth century, and as a result of the ongoing war, Byzantium encouraged the establishment of sericulture in the Levant, which made Byzantium less dependent on Persian raw silk.

The West Arabian route, on the other hand, was used to carry spices which were imported from India and Ceylon, and Yemen's own unique product: frankincense. The Ghassanids were paid to perform essential services for the Meccan caravans along this route: they acted as escorts, offering protection from the attacks of hostile tribesmen, who would be attracted by the rich booty they could get from the caravans; guided the caravans along paths where clear Roman strata did not exist; and supplied them with provisions. Therefore, both Meccans and Ghassanids were on very good terms, and the Meccans had an established history of relying on the Ghassanids' military skills for protection. Such trade slowed down a bit after the capture of Yemen by the Persians and the displacement of the Christian Ethiopians, who were Byzantine allies.

In addition to the two major land routes, there was also a maritime route that ended at Ayla (the modern Eilat) which was controlled by the Ghassanids. Ayla was for centuries a Christian Arab Nabatean town whose inhabitants became Arab Rhomaioi when Caracalla issued his edict in 212. They continued speaking Arabic. Ayla was important in trade and was referred to as Hadirat al-Bahr (the City of the Sea) in the Qur'an (7:163). Moreover, the covenant that the Prophet Muhammad struck with Yuhanna (John) ibn Ru'ba, the master of Ayla, refers to the security given by the Prophet to the caravans reaching it by land and the ships arriving by sea. This is an example of understandings between the Prophet and Christian Arabs between 628 and 632. By the time of his death, nothing would lead us to believe that there was any ground for a future conflict between Muslim Arabs and Christian Arabs. The opposite was true.

End of Ghassanid Monarchy in 582

The tide began to turn against Byzantium with the Persian conquest and occupation of South Arabia in 570. This development coincided with the souring of Ghassanid-Byzantine relations during the reign of Mundir (569–582), which hit rock-bottom in 580.

During the reign of the emperor Tiberius II (r. 578–82), Mundir's loyalty apparently became suspect. In 581, he was arrested during a visit to Constantinople, at the instigation of Maurice, and deported to Sicily in 582 as soon as Maurice became emperor. Almost immediately upon Mundir's arrest, the Ghassanids led by Mundir's oldest son, Nu'man, rebelled, plundered parts of Syria, and defeated a Byzantine army, killing its dux. Nu'man called for negotiations with Constantinople, was arrested in 584, and stayed under house arrest for years. With both Mundir and his crown prince, Nu'man, out of the picture, the eighty-year-old Ghassanid kingdom disintegrated into fifteen separate phylarchates.

The Lakhmids

The Lakhmids were the counterparts of the Ghassanids in pre-Islamic times in almost every aspect of their life and history. They were foederati of Sasanian Persia in much the same way that the Ghassanids were those of Byzantium. Both their capitals, Hira and Jabiya, were the two great Arab centers of pre-Islamic times.

Both had a strong Arab identity, but as vassals of the two world powers, Byzantium and Persia, they were subject to strong influences, cultural and other, that emanated from the two overlords.

Finally, both exercised some influence on the two Arab Islamic dynasties that came to power after the brief period of the four orthodox caliphs, namely the Umayyads, who were heavily influenced by the Ghassanids, and the Abbasids by the Lakhmids. In their respective capitals, the caliphs of the two Arab Muslim dynasties resided initially and for a short time, the Umayyads in Jabiya and the Abbasids intermittently in Hira. Hence, what has been recorded of one informs the history of the other.

The founder of the dynasty was 'Amr ibn Adi; his son, Imru' al-Qais, the celebrated king whose military exploits are imprinted in the oldest Arabic inscription of 328, was buried at Namara. A third important character was al-Mundir of the fifth century; a fourth was al-Nu'man, the father of the great Mundir, the Alamoundaros of the Greeks, who terrorized Byzantine Syria for some fifty years.

Hira, the capital of the Lakhmids, was a well-known city in pre-Islamic times, celebrated for its palaces, churches, and monasteries. The kings built two monumental palaces that were described in the poetry of the time: al-Khawarnaq and al-Sadir. Mas'udi provides a good description of Hira.

Hira remained for a long time a flourishing center in the Islamic period, especially for music and song. Since it was a city of many churches (at least four based on archeological evidence) and monasteries (at least thirty-nine), it could not be a capital for the Islamic caliphate. Hence the building of an entirely new city nearby, Kufa.

However, Hira remained a major Arab center, and when the Abbasids came to power, they enlarged and reused its celebrated royal palace, al-Khawarnaq.

Although the three early Abbasid caliphs (al-Saffāḥ, al-Mansur, and Harun al-Rashid) visited and stayed in Hira. It was Harun who seriously considered Hira a capital or at least a major caliphate residence, according to Tabari. That Harun would consider using Hira as his capital should not be surprising. Hira was the greatest Arab city in Iraq, with a continuous existence of some five hundred years with a distinguished history in both pre-Islamic and Islamic times.

In their capacity as Persian foederati, the Lakhmids built a fearsome army using Persian tactics and weapons. Hira's army had two military divisions: armored cavalry units (al-Shahba') designed to harry enemy infantry in open terrain, and infantry (al-Dawsar) which primarily was used to man forts. Many of the Lakhmid kings were sung as great warriors.

The Lakhmids maintained a heavy military presence not only in Hira but also in many fortresses along the Euphrates opposite Byzantine forts primarily manned by Ghassanid soldiers.

End of Lakhmid Monarchy in 602

Around 602, the Persian king Khosrow II had Nu'man, the king of Hira, murdered because he had converted to Christianity and then, some years later, insisted on complete independence from Persia. This made Khosrow suspicious, and he probably believed that Nu'man's next move was to ally himself with Ghassanid tribes creating a large

Arab kingdom which could be more difficult to manage. At any rate, the death of Nu'man terminated any hope for a consolidated Christian Arab kingdom as well as the history of the dynasty that had ruled Hira for some three hundred years. Khosrow then appointed governors from 602 until his death in 628. Chaos and confusion slowly increased after the death of Nu'man until it erupted in total insurrection against Persia upon Khosrow's death, several years before the Arab conquest.

CHAPTER THREE

Insurrection and Conquest

We will start this chapter by providing a concise review of major events from 502 to 613, the starting date of the Persian occupation of Syria and Palestine. This will highlight certain trends that will help us understand what occurred after the end of the Persian Wars in 628.

We will describe the dynamics that impacted the Middle East in general and Arabia in particular during the Persian occupation of the Levant and Egypt.

We will then use the conclusions we derived from the first two chapters to illuminate the most probable course of events during the crucial years from 628 to 636.

Timeline from 502 to 613

In 502, Anastasius (r. 491–518), in preparation for a campaign against the Sasanians, attracted the Ghassanids to his camp by making them foederati and raising al-Harith ibn Tha'laba to the rank of king. While Anastasius attacked Persia, the Ghassanids attacked Hira, the capital of the Lakhmids, the vassals of the Sasanians.

In 519, a fallout occurred between Jabalah ibn al-Harith and Justin I (r. 518–527). Justin removed the Ghassanids from Byzantine service, who automatically lost all imperial stipends and ability to collect taxes along the trade routes. The majority of Ghassanid troops withdrew from Syria and Southern Palestine and fell back to Northwestern Arabia (Tabuk, Mada'in Saleh, and Ayla), where they camped in and around Christian Arab monasteries from 519 until the death of Justin I in 527.

During their eight-year stay out of Syria, the Ghassanids expanded the monasteries, protected trade from Yemen to Bostra, spread Monophysite Christianity in Arabia, and helped their cousins, the Aws and the Khazraj, get the upper hand against the Jewish tribes of Yathrib, which at the time constituted most of the Yathribi population.

In addition, some Ghassanid troops helped with the Ethiopian invasion of Yemen in 520, which they welcomed, as fellow Christians, after the massacre of Najran Christians by the Jewish Himyarites. This allowed them to further control trade coming from Yemen under friendly Christian Ethiopian control. At this point, the entire Via Odorifera, extending from Yemen to Bostram, was substantially under Ghassanid control as Mecca was under the control of their cousins, the Khuza'a, and Yathrib was now under the control of their cousins, the Aws and Khazraj.

Once Justinian I became emperor (r. 527–565), he immediately restored the Ghassanids to their foederati status. Upon the death of Jabalah in 528, his sons al-Harith and Abu Karib divided Jabalah's dominions between themselves. Al-Harith controlled all of Jordan and Eastern Syria with his capital at Jabiya while Abu Karib controlled Northwestern Arabia and Southern Palestine with his capital at Tabuk.

Justinian I, thinking about starting his own campaign against the Sasanians, promoted al-Harith ibn Jabalah to archphylarch or king of all Arabs in and around the limitrophe of Byzantium.

The years between 530 and 540 were peaceful and prosperous and saw a significant increase in conversions to Christianity along the western coast of Arabia and in Najd, which was controlled by the friendly, mostly Christian, Kindah confederation.

During that period, significant commercial and family ties were developed between the Ghassanids and Mecca's Quraysh.

Then, the second Persian War broke out (540–545). The Ghassanids helped with the entire campaign and continued fighting the Lakhmids until the peace treaty was ratified in 561. At the battle of Chalcis in 554, al-Harith ibn Jabalah killed Mundir, the fearsome king of the Lakhmids.

The plague of Justinian started in 541, at the beginning of the war, and killed several million people in the following twenty-year period. In all, the plague was to kill about forty million people in the two centuries that followed its initial outbreak.

Justinian died in 565 followed by al-Harith ibn Jabalah in 569. Before he died, al-Harith mounted an expedition against the Jews of the Khaybar oasis in support of the Aws and the Khazraj. He was succeeded by his son Mundir.

Justin II (r. 565–578) succeeded Justinian. In 570, the Sasanians invaded Yemen, captured Sana'a and installed Sayf ibn Dhī-Yazan as a vassal. The end of Christian rule in Yemen was an unwelcome event to Byzantium and dealt a blow to trade along the Western Arabia route and reduced both Ghassanid and Meccan profits.

As a direct consequence of the negative impact brought about by the Persian occupation of Yemen and the resulting drop in commerce and tax collection, Mundir asked Justin for an increase in imperial stipends. This angered Justin (a documented miser) so much that he plotted to assassinate Mundir. Thanks to a bureaucratic mix-up, the letter instructing the local Byzantine governor to kill Mundir through treachery was delivered instead to Mundir who, alarmed, left Jabiya and withdrew to Tabuk from 572 until 575.

Most of his troops left for the monasteries of Northwestern Arabia or to camps surrounding Tabuk and Ayla. The timing could not be worse as hostilities with Persia started again in 572 when the Armenians revolted against Sasanian rule. At a stalemate, Justin II recalled Mundir in 575. Back in the fray, the Ghassanids were able to help Maurice, acting as general, and defeat the Sasanians in 578. But acrimony and recriminations between Maurice and Mundir escalated as Mundir, who knew the terrain and was a better general, did not always follow orders and took several initiatives which paid off in 578. Maurice took umbrage at Mundir's independence and laid treason charges against him.

Mundir's record was stellar. He had defeated the Lakhmids and the Sasanians so many times while Maurice achieved little. Tiberius saw that Maurice was acting out of jealousy and instead rewarded Mundir by giving him the title of basileus in 580. Maurice, who was Tiberius's son-in-law and co-emperor, was livid. He finished by convincing dying Tiberius to invite Mundir to Constantinople and then put him under house arrest in 581.

Tiberius died in August 582 and was, as expected, succeeded by Maurice (r. 582–602). One of Maurice's first imperial acts was to exile Mundir to Sicily in 582. Within a few weeks, the oldest son of Mundir, al-Nu'man, rose in revolt, plundered Syria, took over

Byzantine territories, including Bostra, and soundly defeated a Byzantine army sent against him, killing its dux in 582.

For about a year, al-Nu'man ruled two-thirds of Syria, all of Jordan, and the southern part of Palestine, collecting taxes for his own account.

In 584, Maurice invited al-Nu'man to Constantinople for negotiations. Maurice declared his willingness to recall Mundir but only on the condition that al-Nu'man campaigned with the Byzantine forces against Persia with no financial incentive and that he accept the theological formula of Chalcedon.

Al-Nu'man knew that Maurice was in no position to compensate him because his financial situation was very difficult: Maurice ruled a bankrupt empire; it was at war with Persia; he was paying an extremely high tribute to the Avars (80,000 gold solidi a year); and the Balkan provinces were being thoroughly devastated by the Slavs.

Al-Nu'man refused, and he too was arrested and sent to join his father in exile in Sicily. Maurice then changed the Arab policy that had been followed in Byzantium since the time of Justinian. He refused to support any Ghassanid prince for the position of king and even stirred up ill feelings among them. The absence of a unifying figure meant that each one of the fifteen tribes followed its own elected sheikh.

The demise of the Ghassanid federation under Mundir was partially due to his independent character and his role as the protector of the Monophysite Church. In the overwhelmingly pro-Chalcedonian atmosphere of Tiberius's and Maurice's reigns, unlike his father Harith, who was protected by Empress Theodora's Monophysite leanings, Mundir could not count on any influential support in Constantinople.

The Ghassanids left an important cultural legacy. Their patronage of the Monophysite Syrian Church was crucial for its survival and revival, and even its spread, through missionary activities, south into Arabia. According to the historian Warwick Ball, the Ghassanids' promotion of a simpler and more rigidly monotheistic form of Christianity in a specifically Arab context can be said to have anticipated Islam. Ghassanid rule also brought a period of considerable prosperity for the Arabs on the eastern fringes of Syria, as evidenced by a spread of urbanization and the sponsorship of several churches, monasteries, and other buildings.

However, the end of the monarchy and balkanization of the Ghassanids did not mean that the different tribes did not coordinate their positions. They had a permanent majlis (council) at Jabiya. In fact, this new arrangement would backfire against the Byzantines after the end of the Persian occupation in 628.

Away to the east, Shah Khosrow I was also aware of the value of his Lakhmid client allies, and shortly after 531, according to Tabari, made their sheikh, Mundir, king of Oman, Bahrain, and al-Yamama, the northeastern coast of Arabia.

The Sasanian Empire also placed its garrisons in front of the Byzantine ones along their common border and relied on its Arab allies to protect their south flank.

In the end, Khosrow II, like his Byzantine contemporaries, imprisoned King Nu'man in 602 (who had converted earlier to Christianity and, like the Ghassanid Mundir, exhibited a strong streak of independence) and abolished the dynasty, appointing the unknown Iyas ibn Qabisah as governor. The new system was soon tested, since sometime about 609 Banu Bakr and other tribes revolted against Khosrow II and defeated Iyas at the battle of Dhi Qar.

The disbanding the Ghassanid federation significantly weakened Byzantium's protective shield against peninsular Arabs, an error for which the Byzantines would pay dearly with the onset of the Arab conquests. It was paralleled a few years later by the destruction of the Lakhmid kingdom at the hands of the Persians, opening a power vacuum in Northern Arabia, which the nascent Muslim state would later fill.

Events During the Persian Occupation (613–628)

Heraclius came to power in 610 after the demise of Phocas (r. 602–610). The war with Persia started almost immediately. In expectation of the war, Heraclius restored subsidies to the Ghassanids.

But the Ghassanids could not stop the combined Persian and Lakhmid onslaught of 611 on Syria, and Antioch was captured. This essentially cut the Byzantine Empire in half, severing the land connection between Anatolia and Egypt.

At this point, the majority of the Ghassanids (approximately thirty thousand cavalry) withdrew south to Jordan and Tabuk, while a minority withdrew with Byzantine troops to Anatolia.

It should be noted that, by the time Heraclius took over from Phocas, the Byzantine government was in disarray and the treasury was almost empty. To make matters worse, the Avars and Slavs decided to take advantage of the Persian invasion and poured across the northern border raiding Byzantine lands. Heraclius could not afford to divert attention away from Persia, and so had little choice but to buy them off. He paid an annual tribute of 200,000 solidi in exchange for their departure. The size of the Byzantine regular army had dropped to less than fifty thousand.

By 613, all of Syria and Palestine was overtaken. However, Jordan and Northern Arabia stayed under Ghassanid control, as the Persians were overstretched and did not deem it useful or necessary to occupy mostly arid areas and antagonize a mobile force that could harass their supply lines. The Byzantine subsidies to the Ghassanids ceased in 613 as a result of their withdrawal to Jordan and Northern Arabia as well as their ongoing financial difficulties.

Hostilities stopped for five years until 619. This was because the empire was bankrupt and the funds needed to raise and equip a new army could not be found. So Heraclius devalued the currency, stripped Constantinople of its valuables, asked for and received church plate, and declared it the duty of every able-bodied man to fight. New recruits joined with payment of half wages, but with the promise of land grants if reclaimed from the Persians.

In 619, Persia invaded Egypt and stayed there until 629 when they withdrew from both Egypt and Yemen as the civil war was raging back home after its defeat, thanks to the decisive Turkish support provided to Heraclius and the ensuing assassination of Khosrow II in 628.

After Persian withdrawal in 628, most cities and towns were left without garrisons or military commanders. The Ghassanids naturally filled the void. In addition, the Byzantine decision to stop subsidy payments meant that the Ghassanids were effectively given the power to tax since Byzantium knew that they needed income to make up for the lost subsidies. In effect, Byzantium devolved Jordan and the greater part of Syria to the Ghassanids in 628.

This process of devolution had started about forty years earlier but was accelerated by the Persian occupation and significant weakening of Byzantium. We should note that Syria was never as Greek as Greece or Anatolia. Southern Syria was not as Greek as Northwestern Syria

(Antioch). In the early seventh century, the population of Jordan and Southern Syria, including Damascus, was about 60 percent Aramean, 35 percent Arab, 5 percent Kurdish, and less than 1 percent Greek.

It is safe to say that Southern and Eastern Syria and all of Jordan were under full Ghassanid control after 628. Most of Jordan was under Ghassanid control even during the Persian occupation, which never reached less useful and less populated desert areas. From a Byzantine point of view, in 628, the real danger was not external but rather internal emanating from the Ghassanids, who became quasi-autonomous and in full insurrection mode. One can say that the discontinuation of the subsidies and poor treatment of the Ghassanids was a grave Byzantine political and military misstep, which was the primary factor in the loss of Syria and Palestine.

The Crucial Years (628–636)

As stated earlier, the payments to the Turks for their help with the invasion of Mesopotamia in 628 completely dried up the treasury, and Heraclius was not able to resume the subsidies he was paying to the Ghassanids in 628. This act of economy would have dire consequences just a few short months later.

Indeed, the abolition of the subsidies was the last straw that broke the camel's back. While the relationship between Byzantines and their former allies was reaching an all-time low, a significant rapprochement was taking place between the Ghassanids and Muhammad. To better understand the dynamic that occurred between the Ghassanids and Muhammad in 629 and beyond, we need to recap here the existing relationship and its effect on the upcoming events.

The Special Relationship between Ghassanids and Meccans

It is important to describe the close relationship the Ghassanids and the Meccans enjoyed.

The Ghassanids had a strong presence in Mecca through one group of the Azd to which the Ghassanids belonged, Khuza'a, which played an important part in the history of Mecca as custodian of the Kaaba. Qusayy, the great figure in the history of Mecca and ancestor of the Prophet Muhammad, married the daughter of the Khuza'a chief and over time replaced Khuza'a in its dominant role. However, Khuza'a remained a power in Mecca.

In addition, one of the important clans of the Quraysh in Mecca was the Banu Asad ibn 'Abd al-'Uzza, the clan to which belonged Khadija, the first wife of the Prophet Muhammad, and Waraqa ibn Nawfal, the Christian who figured prominently in the early accounts of Muhammad's call to prophethood. The clan was the ally of the Ghassanids in Mecca.

Meccans including Muhammad before his prophetic call and Abu Sufyan, the father of the future caliph Mu'āwiyah, conducted caravans from Mecca over the Via Odorifera, the terminus of which was Bostra, which was controlled by the Ghassanids, who played an important role in the history of this caravan route.

The caravan leaders, including Muhammad, must have had vivid recollections of the power of the Ghassanids at the frontier posts and also in the various fairs (souks) that they presided over, the most important of which were those at Bostra, Adri'at, and Ayyub, all in Provincia Arabia (today's Jordan). Muhammad knew many Ghassanid officials at the fair quite well and developed relationships with them.

During his time as caravan leader for his pro-Ghassanid wife Khadija from the early 580s to the early 590s, an Arab community (*umma*) was already forming between the Ghassanids and the Lakhmids under the loose leadership of the last king of the Lakhmids, al-Nu'man III ibn al-Mundir (r. 580–602). His name was viewed as an omen by the Ghassanids, whose last king was also named al-Nu'man ibn al-Mundir. The Lakhmid al-Nu'man was quite well disposed toward the Ghassanids, so much so that he converted to Christianity in 594.

His conversion cemented a Christian Arab *umma*, which was the talk of the day in the fairs Muhammad attended. Had Muhammad died at that point, a Christian Arab empire would have risen instead of a Muslim one. Therefore, it appears that the notion of umma, as an embodiment of a nascent Arab identity, preceded Islam.

It should also be noted that Ghassanid Monophysite Christianity differed markedly from the Byzantine Chalcedonian creed. Monophysitism (or *wahdaniyyah* in Arabic, "oneness") held that Jesus has only one nature and that nature is divine, not human. The Ghassanids did not view Jesus as the human son of God but rather as the embodiment of the only God Himself walking among us. This theory is exactly the one held by Muhammad, who stated that there was no God but God (Ahadun Ahad). Interestingly, this motto was a Ghassanid one used against the Byzantine Chalcedonians.

As a result, Muhammad never viewed the Ghassanids as *mushrikun* (ones who associate other powers with divinity) because they truly believed in the oneness of God. It was, therefore, natural that they became part of the umma while he was in Yathrib. This meant that Ghassanid soldiers had the same booty rights as Muslims. As we will see later, they were also exempt from the jizya because of their active military service on behalf of the umma.

In addition to the concept of Arab umma and oneness of God, Muhammad borrowed other elements of Ghassanid Christian Arab liturgy such as the use of the visual of a straight Roman road (in this case the Diocletian Strata in Syria which boasts straight-as-an-arrow portions that are miles long each). The Ghassanids coined the phrase "Sirat al-mustaqim" (*sirat* from the Latin word *strata* meaning "path," and *al-mustaqim*, meaning "straight" in Arabic) to describe the righteous path toward God. We find the same phrase (sirat al-mustaqim or straight path) in the first sura of the Qur'an (1–6).

To recap, the Ghassanids were accepting of Muhammad's message, as they viewed Jesus as the embodiment of God on earth and Muhammad was simply speaking, in their own Arabic language, on behalf of God as briefly incarnated by Jesus.

The Ghassanids and Muhammad were very close on many levels: family ties (through Khadija and Khuza'a), language, ethnicity, economics, and religion. By 629, the Ghassanids were much more aligned economically and religiously with Muhammad than they were with the avaricious Chalcedonian Heraclius. The ground was quite ripe for an Arab Ghassanid-peninsular alliance at the end of the Persian War.

The Ghassanid Neutrality

Before we jump to events after the quasi-unification of the Peninsula under Muhammad's leadership by 630, we need first to describe the relationship between the Ghassanids and Muhammad from his Hijra to Medina in 622 until his victory over the Meccans in 628.

I will focus on the Battle of Badr to illustrate such a relationship.

At the time of the Badr battle in early 624, Syria was still under Sasanian occupation and, consequently, the majority of Ghassanid forces were scattered in towns and monasteries around Jordan and Northwestern Arabia. Some of these monasteries were within a day's march from Medina.

As stated earlier, the Ghassanids policed the route leading from Hejaz to the fair at Bostra and provided protection to caravans upon request. We also know that the Aws and Khazraj tribes of Medina, which converted to Islam and became supporters of Muhammad, were Azd cousins of the Ghassanids and, historically, procured their weaponry from them. The Ghassanids controlled two Byzantine *fabricae* in Southern Syria and Northern Jordan and were the primary purveyors of weaponry to the Aws and Khazraj as well as to the Meccans and peninsular Arabs in general.

After the arrival of Muhammad to Medina, his Meccan and other followers also procured their weapons from the same source. It is true that the Ghassanids also sold weaponry to the Meccans. So both parties in the conflict were receiving weapons from the Ghassanids.

However, the Ghassanids stopped short of supporting Muhammad militarily because of their deep commercial ties with Mecca. Muhammad understood that and accepted it.

To further such neutrality, the Ghassanids decided to stop providing security escorts to Meccan caravans on their way to and from the Ghassanid-held fair at Bostra to eliminate any possibility of military conflict with Muhammad's forces.

So when Abu Sufyan (the father of Mu'āwiyah) and future father-in-law of Muhammad learned about Muhammad's plan to attack the caravan, he could not ask for Ghassanid protection, as he would normally, even though he was traveling in their territory north of Medina. He, therefore, was obliged to send messengers all the way south to Mecca asking Abu Jahl for reinforcements. He did so from a location north of Medina under Ghassanid control to eliminate the possibility of an attack while vulnerable and awaiting reinforcements.

Abu Sufyan was right. For the three weeks that it took Abu Jahl to muster reinforcements and reach Badr, which is about 50 miles south of Medina, Muhammad refrained from attacking the caravan. The most likely reason for such restraint is that Abu Sufyan knew that by waiting in a Ghassanid controlled area north of Medina, he was essentially under their protection and knew that Muhammad would not attack him there so as not to antagonize the Ghassanids. It was only once the Meccan reinforcements were on their way that he linked up with Abu Jahl at Badr.

This Ghassanid neutrality will serve them well once Mu'āwiyah (Abu Sufyan's son) became governor of Syria. He remembered that the Ghassanids did not side against his father and would not allow an attack against him before reinforcements arrived.

Ghassanid Insurrection and Support of Peninsular Intervention

The raid of 630 by Muhammad and Khālid ibn al-Walīd into southern Palestine was probably instigated by the Ghassanids, who wanted to use it as a warning to Heraclius so he would relent and resume imperial subsidies. Heraclius did not appear to have received the message or totally ignored it. Consequently, peninsular Arabs found the Ghassanids in a state of absolute resentment and total disloyalty to Byzantium.

It should also be noted that not all of Syria was receptive to Byzantium after the Persian withdrawal. Except for Antioch, the great majority of the inhabitants of Central and Southern Syria were Aramaic or Arabs who did not speak Greek and were not particularly fond of Byzantines. Most Jews preferred the Persians to the Byzantines. Also, most of Syria was left on its own as Constantinople was unable to replenish its garrisons or appoint all needed functionaries by 629. Therefore, there was a power vacuum in Central and Southern Syria that the Ghassanids took advantage of.

The Ghassanids were in full insurrection against Byzantium by 630 and started collecting taxes for their own account to make up for the lack of imperial subsidies. Initially, Byzantium adopted a laissez-faire policy, believing that the insurrection was temporary (it had happened several times in the past). Furthermore, Byzantium lacked the necessary military troops to subdue the Ghassanids. However, by 634, Greek leaders all over Syria and Palestine, who equated illegal tax collection by the Ghassanids to banditry, complained bitterly to the emperor. Sophronius, the new Jerusalem patriarch, added his voice to that of the Byzantine leadership, and finally, Heraclius felt compelled to act.

Battle of Ajnadayn

The Byzantine force was led by Heraclius's own brother Theodore, as well as Vahan, the military commander of Emesa, which was the major Byzantine base of operations in Syria in the early period of the Arab conquests. This encounter, which saw a victory of the Arabs, was called Ajnadayn, meaning "the two armies," which is a clear indication that the Arab contingent was comprised of two separate armies: the Muslim peninsular one and the Christian Ghassanid, both under the overall command of Khālid ibn al-Walīd.

After this victory, the combined Muslim and Christian Arab armies were unopposed in Syria. The subsequent victory at the Battle of Fahl in early 635 cemented Arab military supremacy. The peninsular Arab military advantage was greatly enhanced when Christian Arab tribes who had served imperial armies as regular or auxiliary troops switched sides and joined the West Arabian coalition.

The Byzantines at that point did not differentiate between Arabs: they did not view the enemy as Muslim or Christian but rather as Arab (Saracen). Once the Ghassanids had sided with the peninsular Arabs, and their combined armies went from victory to victory, several Byzantine garrisons recruited from the Syrian Aramean population followed suit: as an example, records indicate that in 635, some four thousand Aramean soldiers under their Byzantine commander Joachim joined the Ghassanids, fellow Christian Monophysites, and helped in the conquest of Syria and later Egypt.

It can be said that by 635, after Ajnadayn, Fahl, and the formal annexation of Bostra and other towns and villages in Southern and Central Syria, including Damascus, the Ghassanids were in full insurrection mode and using their Muslim cousins as a strawman. They were understandably unclear about whether their occupation of the bulk of Syria would last, and just in case the Byzantine would prove able to reconquer it, they decided to use the peninsular Arabs as the culprits if the entire enterprise were to collapse.

Heraclius must have realized that he could not win the conflict militarily, at least not in the short term, and that his only option was to create a chasm between the Ghassanids and their fellow Arab Muslims by narrowing doctrinal differences with Monophysitism and winning back all or some of the Ghassanid forces. Heraclius, therefore, pressured Patriarch Sergius to propagate a new formula, which he hoped would prove acceptable to both Orthodox Chalcedonian Byzantines and Monophysite Ghassanids.

The proposal was that although Christ had two natures, the human and the divine, these natures possessed a single active energy. All that the Ghassanid Monophysites would now be asked to accept was that the unity which they perceived in Christ was one of energy rather than of nature. However, this strategy came to nothing as both Sophronius, the patriarch of Jerusalem since 634, and the Ghassanids completely rejected it for different reasons.

Battle of Yarmuk

Having failed to mend relations religiously with his former allies, Heraclius decided to switch to the military option. Even then, his action was unconvincing. The army he sent in 636 headed by Vahan was only about twenty-thousand strong including auxiliaries. It was faced with an Arab army of approximately the same size. The bulk of the Arab army was Ghassanid and had the advantage of a better knowledge of the terrain and better supplies as Jabiya, their capital, was only a few miles away. There was no way they would face a defeat in their own homeland.

The battle was decided quickly thanks to Ghassanid determination and superior military skills. It certainly never took six days given the accidented terrain which would not accommodate large encampments and the dire lack of water as the Yarmuk stream is almost dry during the month of August.

After the battle of Yarmuk, Caliph Omar made his famous journey to Syria to see the place for himself and to draw up the broad lines of its administration. He chose Jabiya for his headquarters, and it was there that all the Arab commanders came to him and heard his speech, "Khutbat al-Jabiya." The choice of Jabiya by Omar was not fortuitous and was meant to acknowledge Ghassanid help and cement the alliance.

Mu'āwiyah, a few years later, used Jabiya as his capital for the next twenty years. In addition to the choice of Jabiya as capital, he wisely used the help of the Ghassanids, who had helped administer the area for over a century. He could not depend on administrative expertise from Arabia since it did not exist.

All Meccans, including the Umayya clan, were friendly to the Ghassanids, who were fellow Arabs and monotheists. The Ghassanids greatly benefited from the Arab conquest of Syria as they were granted salaries and powerful administrative and military positions and were able to worship freely in accordance with their Monophysite beliefs away from the oppression of Orthodox Chalcedonian Byzantium. In fact, Monophysitism, in many respects, was closer to Islam than it was to Chalcedonian Orthodoxy.

Militarily, during the Umayyad period, the Ghassanids remained deployed in various locations such as Jabiya, Jund al-Urdunn, and Damascus. Their military expertise was needed both internally in the Levant and externally in the campaigns in Anatolia and other fronts. One of its most visible and concrete manifestations was the employment of Hassan ibn al-Nu'man, a Ghassanid general, as head of the campaign for the conquest of North Africa.

Iraq

Similar events occurred in Iraq. After Khosrow's assassination in 628, civil war immediately broke out, which divided Persia among many factions, bled the country, and severely weakened the Sasanian regime. Matters worsened in 630 when the empress Boran came to the throne. It became known among both the Lakhmids and peninsular Arabs that "the Persians no longer have a king, they have sought refuge in a woman," and pillaging accelerated further, sometimes deep into Sasanian territory. These actions went largely unchallenged. So, as was the case in Syria with the Ghassanids, the Lakhmids were in full insurrection and began to take full advantage of the empire's weakness to plunder or tax the outlying areas long before Muhammad's West Arabian coalition became involved.

By 631, the Lakhmids had regained their full independence by getting rid of Azadbeh, the last Sasanian governor, and were in full control of the Hira district, Eastern Arabia, and a portion of the Jazira, the fertile region bound by the Tigris and the Euphrates.

By the time the peninsular Arabs arrived in 633, the Lakhmids had been in a state of full independence for approximately two years. Therefore, the entire Abbasid chronicle of the Battle of Sallasil in 633 under which Khālid ibn al-Walīd defeated Persian armies in today's Kuwait and proceeded to capture Hira is blatantly exaggerated because that entire area was no longer under Sasanian control but rather under the Lakhmids, fellow Arabs, who had no interest in engaging in pitched battle against fellow Arabs while at the same time fending off the Sasanians.

In fact, Khālid ibn al-Walīd walked into Hira unopposed and entered into an agreement with the Lakhmids under which both parties vowed mutual aid and equal division of bounty.

The Persians, of course, were quite surprised and dismayed by the new alliance. However, the Sasanian Empire was paralyzed and incapable of reacting. Yazdegerd, the new boy *shahinshah*, was surrounded by ineffective advisers and was in no position to unite his empire, which was quickly crumbling into small feudal kingdoms which became totally unresponsive to demands for military aid. Even Persian military contingents directly under Yazdegerd's control saw the writing on the wall and decided to switch sides. Some twelve thousand soldiers "converted" to Islam or Christianity in 633 alone and merged with Lakhmid or Rashidun army contingents.

The balkanization of the Sasanian Empire, which started in 629 and was in an advanced stage by 633, became the administrative system of choice for the Arabs, who would rely on the small rural nobility (the *dihqans*, the petty landholding nobility which was the backbone of later Sasanian provincial administration and tax collection) to control the countryside in exchange for lower taxes and total freedom in local affairs. This explains why the Arabs did not create a single mişr in Kirman, Khorasan, or Tabaristan, while they created three in Iraq (Kufa, Basra, and Wasit) where the dihqan feudal system did not exist.

As in the case of Syria with the Ghassanids, the Christian Lakhmids kept substantial autonomy and power under the Umayyads and continued to account for most of the scribes, leaders, and governors.

Evolving Composition of Rashidun Army

The Rashidun army was the core of the Rashidun Caliphate's armed forces during the conquests. Its size was initially 13,000 men in 632 and increased to 18,000 in 633, 41,000 in 634, and 70,000 by 636.

The initial 13,000 was the maximum number peninsular Arabs could contribute demographically, as the entire population of the Arabian Peninsula amounted to only approximately 150,000. About 100,000 were male due to the widespread practice of female infanticide. Able-bodied men between the ages of eighteen and thirty-five amounted to approximately 25,000. The contingent of 13,000 men meant that half of all able-bodied men were circumscribed or volunteered.

Such numbers could not perform the conquest, especially since the great majority never fought with anything besides a stick and didn't own swords, a mount, or even footwear. Therefore, peninsular Arabs relied on Christian Arabs and massive "conversions" of Syrians,

Byzantines, and Persians who ended up outnumbering peninsular Arabs five to one by 636 and ten to one by 640.

To make matters worse, as most peninsular Arabs lived for generations in isolation and self-sufficiency in the Arabian desert, they lacked antibodies against the plague and other diseases. So as they emerged from Arabia into Syria, they became easy prey for the plague. In 639, two-thirds of the 10,000 strong peninsular Arab army in Syria perished within a matter of two months, including its commander and then governor of Syria Yazid ibn Abi Sufyan.

This prompted the second caliph, Omar, to appoint Yazid's younger brother, Mu'āwiyah, as the new governor. Fearing a Byzantine invasion that would have easily retaken Syria, Mu'āwiyah promptly married Maysun, the daughter of Bahdal ibn Unayf, the preeminent sheikh of the Arab Christian Kalb tribe (a Ghassanid tribe), to further strengthen his alliance with the Ghassanids.

Bahdal himself remained Christian until his death in 657. This heavy reliance on Ghassanid Christian tribes created much confusion and a major rift within the decimated army ranks, and a Byzantine counterattack would have been successful.

During the conquest of Egypt (641–644), 'Amr ibn al-'As engaged in mass conversions of Christian Copts so they could be recruited. Similarly, during the conquest of North Africa, Berber converts to Islam were recruited as regular troops. These converts accepted Islam not necessarily because of immediate belief in a religion they did not understand, but rather because of the collapse of their own societies and natural willingness to align with the winners so they could secure their future.

This process meant that by the 660s, the number of peninsular Arabs anywhere had dropped below one hundred thousand. Little by little, the composition of the Rashidun army shifted gradually from peninsular Arab to mostly Christian Arab and finally to non-Arab with a significant future impact on the cohesion and unity of the expanding empire.

CONCLUSION

The Abbasid Muslim storyline that the conquests were fully planned and managed by the Prophet and his successors is largely incorrect. The Arab (not Muslim) conquests were not initiated by the Prophet alone but had begun before him in the form of local insurrections by the Christian Ghassanids in Syria and the Christian Lakhmids in Iraq.

The righteous community (*umma*) formed by Muhammad in Medina had as a primary mission to wage jihad against the unrighteous (*mushrikun*) who are defined in the Qur'an as those who denied God's oneness. The agreement that Muhammad made in Medina was a mutual defense pact and a war manifesto by the believers in the One God against those who did not. It did not matter whether the believers in the One God were Muslim or Christian. They were on equal footing. The term for a treaty signatory was *mu'min*, meaning "faithful" (to the treaty). As with the English word *faithful*, *mu'min* could mean both loyal and believing. So the *mu'minun* were not only Arab Muslims but also Arab Christians who likewise believed in the oneness of God and readily accepted Muhammad, a fellow Arab and a sage, as the supreme arbiter of the umma.

Muhammad's umma was, then, pluralist in nature, with everyone committed to waging jihad against the pagans (the Persians certainly were and the Byzantines by believing in a duality were certainly not monotheists in the eyes of the Ghassanids or Muhammad), whatever their own monotheist persuasion.

Later Muslim historians played down this pluralist dimension and the Arab Christian role, seeking to portray the conquests as a purely Muslim venture. Further proof that Muslim Arabs were not the main actors in the conquests is that there were no rank-and-file sung heroes. At the time of the crusades, over three centuries after the conquests, when Arabs needed to sing the feats of historical heroes to give them courage against the invading Christians, they bypassed the conquests with its battles against those very Christians and reached back into the pre-Islamic period and selected Antara ibn Shaddad (the pagan mythical hero of the Dāhis and Ghabrā War) as the quintessential Arab war hero.

The umma had two primary objectives, one spiritual and the other materialistic. The spiritual objective involved the creation of a unifying framework emphasizing the oneness of God, which was the common denominator linking all Arabs at the time, whether Muslim or Christian. And by displaying a unified front against the pagan Persians and the dualist Byzantines (the mushrikun), the umma placed more weight on the Arabness of the community creating a new identity that transcended clan and tribe for the first time.

Both Ghassanids and Lakhmids were predisposed to accepting a unity under a common Arab arbiter: They were both used to a unifying royal model and missed the destruction of their dynasties by their Byzantine and Persian overlords. Here was an opportunity to rectify that.

In addition, Christian Arabs were first and foremost Arabs who were very proud of their common Arab heritage and language. Nothing pleased them more than good Arabic poetry. And hence, like any other Arab, they greatly appreciated the beautiful poetry inherent in the Qur'an.

Even today, fourteen centuries later, I, an atheist, am moved by the music of the Qur'an, an emotion that brings tears to my eyes and confounds my rational side. You can then imagine the power a recitation of the Qur'an had on Christian Arabs back then.

The Ghassanids would not fight their brethren and would not defend an emperor who would not pay them, would not speak to them, called them Saracens, and viewed them as heretics. What the Ghassanids wanted was not the perpetuation of a racist, arabophobic, and ungenerous Byzantine rule, but the opportunity to self-rule and worship freely in accordance with their Monophysite beliefs. But faith was not the only instigator of Christian insurrection and Muslim intervention in the Levant and Iraq. The other objective was simply self-enrichment as allowed by God.

It should be noted that the concept of reward in the Qur'an evolved from the Meccan period where the bulk of the rewards were to be received in the afterlife to the Medina period where a larger emphasis was placed on rewards to be received on this earth. This certainly galvanized and incentivized both peninsular and Christian Arabs. At around the time the umma was being formed, the Qur'an became very explicit about the rewards that those who fight the mushrikun can expect in this life: "God has promised that you will take much booty and He has expedited this for you" (48:20), so "consume the booty that you have captured as a lawful benefit" (8:69).

These exhortations were very much in line with the predisposition of both Ghassanids and Lakhmids, who for so long relied on booty and subsidies for income as well as with the temperament of the peninsular Bedouins inclined to raiding and plundering and Quraysh's inclination to trading and toll taking as traditional guardians of the holy shrine in Mecca.

The "business plan" underlying the conquests was to plunder, use a portion of the proceeds to hire sham converts, pushed either by fear or self-ambition, to swell their ranks; conquer populations, and then impose jizya, a poll tax. Note that converting conquered populations would dilute the gains from plunder because they would have to be shared with a larger group. Therefore, the point of the conquest was not to convert the conquered to the new faith but just to impose the poll tax on them. The poll tax was essentially a protection tax based on the notion that people not belonging to the umma (Muslim and Christian Arabs) cannot fight, and therefore it becomes incumbent upon Arabs to provide such protection. The jizya proceeds were then used to pay off the troops and hire enough converts to expand conquest territories. The Umayyads excelled at this game: they used jizya and plunder to finance a standing army and pay annual pensions to all able-bodied Arabs (Muslim or Christian) who fought or were in active reserve.

Therefore, there was little interest in converting pagan Persians or Syrian Aramean Christians (and later Egyptian Christian Copts) as that would have reduced jizya proceeds. Proof is that by the ascension of the Abbasids to power in 750, about 70 percent of Aramean Syrians and 90 percent of Copts in Egypt were still Christian and 95 percent of Persians were still Zoroastrian. It goes without saying that both Ghassanids and Lakhmids stayed largely Christian because they were exempt from the jizya.

In fact, the word *conquest* does not properly describe the facts on the ground. Given the low numbers of Arabs and the fact that they were concentrated in few garrison camps (amṣar) from which they exercised military control (with the caliph, his governors, and associated courts ensconced in large palace compounds), the great majority of "conquered" peoples never saw a single Arab (Muslim or Christian), and you could walk around Syria, Iraq, and Persia for days or weeks without realizing that such territories were conquered. A far cry from those wide swaths of green all over Middle East maps in the history textbooks showing the extent of control of the presumed new Muslim empire. The truth is that the conquests resulted in a tenuous hold on largely self-administered Christian and Zoroastrian lands.

The overthrow of the Umayyads was primarily due to the failure of the business plan and the resulting bankruptcy of the treasury: inability to raid more territory in Europe (resounding defeat of Poitiers in 732) or in Asia Minor to get more plunder and rebellion of most of the *dihqans* in Eastern Persia who stopped paying jizya. These two factors combined emptied the treasury and did not allow the Umayyads to continue paying the annual pensions to the Arab tribes and hire Turkish, Berber, and Byzantine mercenaries to stop the Abbasid rebellion.

The discontinuation of the payment of pensions to Arab tribes was probably the beginning of the end for the Umayyads. The pension system was introduced in 637 by Caliph Omar and was therefore viewed as sacrosanct. A register of all adults who could be called to war was prepared, and a scale of salaries was fixed. All registered men were liable for military service. They were divided into two categories, namely those who formed the regular standing army and those that lived in their homes but were liable to be called whenever needed. The pay was given in cash at the beginning of the month of Muharram, the first month in the Muslim calendar. In contrast to many post-Roman polities in Europe, grants of land were of only minor importance.

It is interesting to note that while Muslims did not mind jizya-paying non-Muslims during the good times, they were in the habit of attributing public calamities to non-Muslims who were angering

Allah by their mere existence. On the occurrence of famine or pestilence, the mob invariably broke into violence against Christians, Jews, and pagans.

Jizya and plunder were of paramount importance to the treasury as commerce substantially collapsed. Prior to the conquest, Syria had a flourishing trade with Byzantium and with places as far as Marseille. The records of the port of Marseille show that trade with Syria collapsed as Arabs confiscated merchant ships for the war effort, or at least the ones that did not escape as Arabs besieged the main port of Caesarea Maritima. The archeological records show that the city was largely destroyed upon conquest in 640. And with that, trade and associated taxes disappeared. The exact same story happened in Alexandria around the same time. The great majority of rich traders from Syria and Egypt escaped to Constantinople.

The transfer of booty in the form of gold coins from surrendering cities to the benefit of Arabs, both Christian and Muslim, resulted in a severe shortage of liquidity and associated negative impact on commerce. The plague of 639 created further economic upheaval at the worst possible time as craftsmen and farmers died in the tens of thousands, severely curtailing production and economic activity.

As the economy in Syria and Egypt collapsed, the only remaining government revenue was jizya and plunder, in that order. Mu'āwiyah tried to expand plunder by occupying the Aegean Islands and even besieging Constantinople for seven years (672–679) hoping to ransack the city and its riches. But the venture failed. During the period from 635 until 685, the economy was so poor that the Umayyads could not afford to mint their own coinage and relied on the Byzantine solidus, the currency of the enemy they were trying to vanquish.

The focus on Constantinople and its superior riches caused the drive toward poorer North Africa to be paused from the 660s through the

680s. The restart of the drive in 697 was not targeting poor North Africa but rather richer Western Europe now that the invasion from the East had failed.

This explains why the Arabs made a beeline for Carthage in order to create a miṣr close by (Kairouan) and then proceeded directly to Tangier where they arrived in 700. Instead of occupying the vast empty expanses of Morocco and Algeria, they focused on rallying Berber tribes to mount the first raid against Spain in 710. Once they realized that their intuition was correct, they mounted the larger expedition of 711 which resulted in much more plunder, some of which was sent to Damascus in 713 in an enormous caravan.

No thought was given to creating a miṣr in Algeria or Morocco. Effective Islamization of Morocco did not start until after the arrival of Idris ibn Abdillah, the great-great-great grandson of the Prophet, who arrived sometime after 780 and founded the Idrisid dynasty in 788. His seat was at Volubilis, a dilapidated Roman border town, since no miṣr or Muslim town was ever built by the "conquering" Arabs in the eighty years that preceded his arrival.

The plunder expansion continued after the occupation of most of Spain. The first small raids against Narbonne, Bordeaux, were so lucrative in the 720s that they mounted the larger raid against Northern France when they failed at Poitiers in 732.

The Umayyads quickly faded away once territorial expansion slowed down and with it plunder and jizya proceeds. The Abbasids, in turn, were all but forgotten by 900, about 150 years after their ascent to power as jizya collapsed because of massive conversions of Persians, Syrians, and Egyptians and the loss of plunder proceeds. This allowed the balkanization of the Islamic world (Idrisids, Aghlabids, Fatimids, Samanids, etc.)

Another reason for the demise of the Umayyads was the marginalization of its Christian support base. In the beginning, the Umayyads displayed both Muslim and Christian leanings and were well disposed toward the Ghassanids and accepted them both as fellow Arabs and as Christian monotheists, followers of Jesus, a holy figure in the Qur'an.

The Umayyad caliph Yazid, the son of Mu'āwiyah, even entrusted the education of his son Khalid to a monk named Istephan. Yazid himself was the son of a Christian mother, Maysun, the daughter of the phylarch of the tribe of Kalb. It should be noted that Kalb and other Ghassanid tribes became extremely important militarily after peninsular troops, who had little immunity to the plague, were decimated by the famous plague of Amwas, which broke out in 638–639. The Arab Christians had much better immunity, as they had experienced it in 592, 599, 607, and sometime between 612 and 617.

The first signs of Islamization occurred under Abdel Malik in 692 after he was forced to kill Abdallah ibn Zubayr and put down his rebellion in the Hejaz. Abdallah's paternal grandmother was Safiyyah bint Abd al-Muttalib, the paternal aunt of Muhammad, and his mother was Asma, a daughter of the first caliph, Abu Bakr (r. 632–634), and sister of A'isha, a wife of Muhammad. Abdallah was also the first child born to the Muhajirun in Medina in 624. These links to Muhammad, who used to hold him on his knees and stroke his hair, endeared him to Muslims and enhanced his reputation throughout his life. Abdallah claimed that the Umayyads were not true Muslims (he was quite right about that), and his killing by al-Hajjaj turned many Muslims against the Umayyads, who were forced to show outward signs of Islam. Hence, there was the pretense of an Islamization of the regime through Arabization of the administration and the introduction of new coinage displaying fervent religious mottos such as the inscription, "There is no God but God; He has no equal."

But the harm was done, and rebellions continued. After the death of al-Hajjaj in 714, the situation became untenable. The Umayyads felt that they needed to show their Muslim devotion by finally getting serious about conquering Byzantium. So, after years of preparation, in 717, they invaded Anatolia and sent a huge fleet to besiege Constantinople.

The entire plan backfired. The siege was a total disaster, especially after the Bulgar intervention in Thrace. This failure was proof to most Muslims that the Umayyads were no longer favored by God and further reinforced the notion that they were not true Muslims and did not deserve to rule.

The defeat also created a backlash against Christian Arabs both in Syria and Iraq and heralded the waning of Christian Arab influence. Such influence totally disappeared by the Umayyads' overthrow by the Abbasids and their Persian supporters. From then onward, the umma was strictly viewed as Muslim, and the re-writing of history began.

EPILOGUE

T he imagery of greatness, past splendor, and power planted by the orientalists helped cradle Arabs' hope in the impossible.

Arab nationalists, with no small help from orientalists, citing false accounts from late Muslim chroniclers, created generations of Arabs believing that a glorious past was stolen from them through treachery, and that a combination of true faith, as existed at the time of the Prophet, and violence will help them regain their exalted past glory. Thus, a cult of the hero was created depicting peninsular Arabs at the time of the Prophet all the way to today's Palestinian guerillas passing by Barbary corsairs, as sung war heroes.

Unfortunately, Muslim Arab achievements were greatly exaggerated, and those false beliefs made sure that nostalgia took precedence over modernity and innovation.

As the tables turned and both Americans and Europeans were finally able first to push back (effective end of piracy in the Atlantic and Mediterranean in 1815) and then take the offensive starting in the 1820s with the support of Greek independence against the combined Ottoman and Egyptian forces, Arabs started developing a narrative of victimhood. The cult of the victim took on enormous proportions as the defeat of Morocco at the hands of Spain in 1860 was followed by the conquest of Tunisia in 1881, Egypt in 1882, Libya in 1911, Morocco in 1912, and Syria and Iraq in 1919. The fall of the

Ottoman Caliphate in 1924 signaled the end of an era and showed the cult of the victim in full bloom.

One can imagine how Arabs felt, tugged between a lionized past and a miserable present, between a depiction of their forefathers as heroes while they viewed themselves as victims of a new world they could not understand and make their own. Indeed, the current power of the cult of the victim derives from the sharp contrast with the mythologized golden age and the associated cult of the hero.

The clinging to a false historical narrative and the feeling of victimhood had the effect of having Arabs cling to the comfort of their religious dogma, which further inhibited them from joining modernity. They are now spectators believing that they could have been actors if not for Zionist and neo-colonialist plots. Failed societies and economies pushed young men and women to either migrate to the West and/ or engage in religious righteousness with a slippery slope toward extremism and terrorism. It is crucial that the historical record be reviewed and corrected so that Arabs can finally let go of nostalgia for a false glorious past and focus on shaking their dogmas and dictators and look forward to a brighter future.

Arabs need to get rid of both cults and seek a realistic middle way through dialogue and realization that all civilizations, including their own, are the product of many contributions, including those of their supposed enemies. That is why Arabs need to open up and embrace their supposed enemies and oppressors. We need a new umma replicated along the pluralist model Muhammad so wisely designed, which includes Muslims, Christians, and Jews. The first step toward this goal is to highlight Christian Arab contributions to the umma and to Arab civilization and integrate Christian Arab history in the fabric of Arab history. Countries such as Lebanon, Syria, Iraq, and Egypt, with their significant and vibrant Christian minorities, should lead the way. All Arab countries should allow their citizens to choose the religion of their choice and, in doing so, making it a personal choice, not a state-imposed one.

This act of tolerance and inclusion is the necessary first step toward openness and acceptance of the other, which can broaden the Arab mind and promote multidimensional thinking and creativity. A meaningful religious dialogue based on acceptance and mutual respect may allow a new unifying Jerusalem to rise making possible the creation of a new common foundation upon which much deeper religious, social, cultural, and economic cooperation can thrive to the benefit of all.

Muslims should not hark back to the black flag of the Abbasids (symbol of ISIS) but rather to the white flag of the Umayyads, a symbol of peace and tolerance, values that allowed the harnessing of talents and efforts of both Christians and Muslims toward a common objective.

The Qur'an argues repeatedly that all religious systems associated with the Peoples of the Book should not only be respected but should be viewed as equivalent beliefs that will all grant their adherents equal access into the world to come: "Believers, Jews, Christians, and Sabaeans—whoever believes in God and the last Day and who work righteousness: they have their reward with their Lord, they shall not fear nor should they grieve" (2.62; see also 5:69 and 22:17).

It is hoped that this new umma will heal current wounds, close glaring gaps, and revive ancient bonds. Only together building on our common past and looking forward to a shared future can we hope to create lasting understanding, prosperity, and peace.

The power of the cult of the victim derives from the mythology surrounding the cult of the hero. To defeat the former, we need first to address the latter. We therefore need to realistically reassess the mythologized golden age starting from the very beginning: the Arab conquests.

Arabs cannot imagine their future without first reassessing their past. This will allow them to accept the huge contributions others made, accept that globalization has been at work for a long time, and that as before, there is a place for them, their culture, and their language alongside the others'.

As Arabs navigate the gray between the extreme cults of heroism and victimhood, they will inevitably have to deal with complexities and fading certainties. They will need to embrace the universal, whether relating to democracy or human rights, and stop believing in a supposed Arab exception.

SELECT BIBLIOGRAPHY

Agha, S. S. *The Revolution Which Toppled the Umayyads: Neither Arab nor Abbasid* (Leiden, 2003).

Baladhuri, *Futuh al-buldan*, ed. M. J. de Goeje (Leiden, 1866).

Bashear, S. *Arabs and Others in Early Islam* (Princeton, 1997).

Crone, P., and Cook, M. *Hagarism: The Making of the Islamic World* (Cambridge, 1977).

Donner, F. *The Early Islamic Conquests* (Princeton, 1980).

Haldon, J. *Byzantium in the Seventh Century* (2nd revised edition: Cambridge, 1997).

Howard-Johnston, J. *Witnesses to a World Crisis* (Oxford, 2010).

Hoyland, R. G. *Arabia and the Arabs* (London, 2001).

Hoyland, R. G. *In God's Path* (Oxford, 2015).

Ibn Ishaq, *The Life of Muhammad*, Trans, A. Guillaume, 1955. (Reprint, Karachi, 1990).

Ibn Khaldun, Muqaddimah (Beirut, 1956).

John of Nikiu, *Chronicle*, trans. R. H. Charles (London, 1916).

Kennedy, H. *The Great Arab Conquests* (Cambridge, MA, 2007).

Lewis, B. *The Arabs in History* (New York, 1957).

Maurice's Strategikon: Handbook of Byzantine Military Strategy. Trans. G. Dennis (Philadelphia, 1984).

Nicolle, D. *The Great Islamic Conquests* (Oxford, 2009).

Peters, F. E. *The Arabs and Arabia on the Eve of Islam* (Variorum; Aldershot, 1999).

Rosenthal, F. *A History of Muslim Historiography* (Leiden, 1968).

Sartre, M. Bostra, *Des Origines a l'Islam* (Paris, 1985).

Shahid, I. *Byzantium and the Arabs in the Sixth Century* (Washington, DC, 1984-2009).

Tabari, *Ta'rikh al-rusul wa-l-muluk*, ed. M. J. de Goeje et al. (Leiden, 1879-1901).

Tannous, J. *Syria between Byzantium and Islam* (PhD; Princeton, 2010).

Wood, P. *We Have No King but Christ: Christian Political Thought in Greater Syria on the Eve of the Arab Conquest* (Oxford, 2010).

Ya'qubi, *Ta'rikh 2*, ed. M. T. Houtsma (Leiden, 1883).

Made in United States
North Haven, CT
08 June 2024

53353767R00061